M000218836

The Flowing Bridge

Eternal gratitude
to the consummate Source
of life, and light, and love.

The Flowing Bridge

Guidance on Beginning Zen Koans

Elaine MacInnes

Edited by Patrick Gallagher

Foreword by Ruben L.F. Habito

Wisdom Publications
199 Elm Street
Somerville MA 02144 USA
www.wisdompubs.org

© 2007 Elaine MacInnes
All rights reserved.

No part of this book may be reproduced in any form or by any
means, electronic or mechanical, including photography, recording,
or by any information storage and retrieval system or technologies
now known or later developed, without permission in writing from
the publisher.

Library of Congress Cataloging-in-Publication Data
MacInnes, Elaine.
  The flowing bridge : guidance on beginning Zen koans / Elaine MacInnes ;
foreword by Ruben L. F. Habito ; edited by Patrick Gallagher.
    p. cm.
  ISBN 0-86171-545-4 (pbk. : alk. paper)
  1. Koan. 2. Spiritual life—Zen Buddhism. I. Habito, Ruben L. F., 1947- II.
Gallagher, Patrick C., 1951– III. Title.
  BQ9289.5,M33 2007
  294.3'927—dc22
                                        2007021082

First Edition
11 10 09 08 07
5 4 3 2 1

Cover design by Rick Snizik. Interior design by Dede Cummings.
Set in Caslon 11.5/15.5. Cover calligraphy "Flow" by Michael Milburn.

Wisdom Publications' books are printed on acid-free paper and meet the guidelines for permanence and durability of the Production Guidelines for Book
Longevity of the Council on Library Resources.

Printed in the United States of America

♻ This book was produced with environmental mindfulness. We have elected
   to print this title on 50% PCW recycled paper. As a result, we have saved
the following resources: 19 trees, 13 million BTUs of energy, 1,651 lbs. of green-
house gases, 6,854 gallons of water, and 880 lbs. of solid waste. For more information, please visit our website, www.wisdompubs.org.

Contents

Foreword
Invitation to an Inward Journey

The Zen experience of *kensho*, or "seeing one's true nature," is a pivotal point in a practitioner's spiritual path. For some it can be a spectacular event that takes them entirely by surprise, accompanied by spontaneous outbursts of laughter or tears, or even both. For others it can be quiet, internal and unobtrusive—yet nonetheless momentous and life-changing. In any case, a genuine awakening experience marks a significant shift in a person's view of self, of the world, of reality.

This awakening experience, crucial as it is, however, tends to be romanticized, idealized, and overemphasized in some popularized accounts of Zen. It can be depicted in ways that give a rather misleading impression of what Zen is all about.

The awakening experience is set in better perspective if we look at it in context as one of the "three fruits" of Zen practice and the Zen way of life. These are, first, deepening the "power of single-minded concentration" (*joriki,* in Japanese)," second, *kensho,* and third, "the embodiment of the peerless way" *(mujo do no taigen).*

This first fruit of Zen is about "con-centration." Here I use the word deliberately with a hyphen, to differentiate it from the usual meanings of the word "concentration," emphasizing that it has to do with "coming together toward the center of one's being," or "center-ing." In other words, as you continue and deepen your Zen practice, the disparate pieces of your life will begin to come together, and you will be able to move in the direction of a greater integration of the various facets of your life and your being. From a condition of being dispersed and rootless, you will learn how to be centered and grounded, in all that you are and do. More or less, that is, for you can always run into snags, backslide a little, or fall into lapses along the way.

Yet even with the inevitable twists and turns, or ups and downs, you will nevertheless begin to have a deeper appreciation of what it is "just to be," and not feel always measured by how you perform in others' eyes or by the results of what you do. You will tend to be less concerned by thoughts of meeting certain ideals, or by the pressure of conforming to the expectations of others, and so on. Rather, you will be enabled to go about your tasks with a greater sense of inner freedom, able to be more truly yourself, "just as you are."

The first fruit can begin to take effect in a practitioner's life within a short time after engaging in seated meditation practice (zazen) on a regular basis. You will find a sense of greater focus in the various things you normally do in daily life. You will learn more and more how to live mindfully, and develop a capacity to be in the moment, able to simply relish each sight, sound, smell, taste, touch, and thought that comes up—just as it is.

As you continue Zen practice, enjoying the different manifestations of this first fruit in your life, there may come a moment, unexpected, unprepared for, when you are hit by a sudden flash of realization. "This is it!" As noted above, this could be a spectacular event accompanied by "fireworks," or it could be a quiet, externally unremarkable, simple moment of recognition—*Aha!* It is a moment that ushers in deep peace, unfathomable joy, inexplicable gratitude. The experience of awakening entails all the above. This is the second fruit of Zen practice, of the Zen way life.

Each individual comes to this experience in a mode that is unique and unrepeatable, with different degrees of intensity and from varying points of entry. It can be a visual stimulus, such as the sight of a flower, the clear blue sky, or a tree stump. It can be a sound, such as the ticktock of a clock, a musical note, a bell, the bark of a dog, the chirp of a bird. It can be tactile, such as the whack of the encouragement stick on the back while sitting in the meditation hall, the sudden pain felt as an unshod toe hits a pebble on an unpaved walkway, or a soothing massage on a stiff shoulder.

This is a refreshing, breathtaking, and exhilarating experience indeed. It can be like floating up in the sky, free as a feather. It is an experience that brings forth tremendous joy, as it opens you to a glimpse of the infinite horizon of your own being, the vast unfathomable riches of your own True Self. *Kensho* is a realization, in all immediacy, of what the Heart Sutra affirms: Form is no other than Emptiness, Emptiness no other than Form.

Yet, as it is an initial glimpse into such untold vistas, such an experience can tend to make you lose your bearings, and become somewhat disoriented. It can dislocate you, or cause what you thought was the solid ground under your feet to disintegrate. It is like having the rug pulled from under you, making you lose balance, maybe even knocking you flat on your face. You can easily get disoriented, lost, in the vastness and infinite horizons of Emptiness, and find it hard to come down to earth, back to daily life and its ordinariness.

At this point there can be a tendency in those graced with this initial glimpse to want to hold on to it, to stay there and continue to float in those dizzying heights. This is where the phenomenon called *Zen sickness* can take hold. The "discovery" of this world of Emptiness can be so exciting that the practitioner talks about it all the time to everyone around, saying how wonderful it is, and so on, without regard for the persons being addressed or the situations in which such talk is imposed.

Also, soon after the glimpse of Emptiness, the delusive mind can again come in and "claim" even that as a prized possession, and perhaps put it in a neat little frame to hang on the wall. "I've got it" or "I'm enlightened." And the very moment that such thoughts come, you have separated yourself from it. The more philosophically inclined will find it hard to resist waxing profound on the tremendous conceptual implications of the notion of Emptiness and how it relates to the world of Form, and so on. Zen sickness can take various modes and come in varying degrees of intensity, some kinds taking a longer time to overcome than others.

There is a word in Spanish, *aterrizar,* used in referring to airplanes as they gradually approach the earth *(terra)* and land safely on the ground. This term is most apt to describe what needs to happen to a Zen practitioner after kensho. The third fruit of Zen practice is about this process of touching ground again, after soaring the lofty heights of the vast Empty sky. It involves a process not only of finding the ground, but also of taking root, and blossoming, and bearing fruit in abundance, fruits of wisdom and compassion actualized in daily life. It is a never-ending journey that continues throughout life.

This third fruit relates to the actualization of the awakening experience in all that it entails in every nook and cranny of daily life. While the second fruit may take but a moment, the flash of an instant, to manifest itself, the cultivation and maturation of this third fruit takes an entire lifetime. The glimpse of the infinite horizons of your True Self, given in the initial awakening experience, can leave you dazed and dislocated, and it can take some time to be able to land safely back on earth again, to return to your normal senses.

This is why continuing practice after the initial awakening experience is essential in a practitioner's life.

In our Sanbo Kyodan lineage—based on the teaching and practice of three founding Zen masters, Daiun Harada (Great Cloud), Haku'un Yasutani (White Cloud), and Koun Yamada (Cultivating Cloud), who together form the "Three Clouds" (San-un) of our home practice place, San-un Zendo, located in Kamakura, Japan—we have this small treasure box called the Miscellaneous Koans, culled from the various koan collections handed down from the Zen Masters of China, Korea, and Japan. A practitioner confirmed in the kensho experience is given a little booklet with this collection of miscellaneous koans, as the next stage of practice, to help in the process of settling back on the ground again. It contains twenty-two items, many of which have subheadings. For a practitioner who goes regularly to the face-to-face meetings *(dokusan)* with the teacher to "work" on these miscellaneous koans, it may take from several weeks to several months, or up to a year or two, to go through this collection.

After having worked through this initial set of assorted koans, the practitioner is led koan by koan through the major collections, the *Wu-men Kuan (Mumonkan)* or Gateless Gate, the *Piyen Lu (Hekigan-roku)* or Blue Cliff Record, the *Ts'ung jung lu (Shoyoroku)* or the Book of Equanimity, the *Denko-roku* or Record of Transmitting the Light, and, as the capstone, the Five Ranks, the Pure Precepts, and the Ten Grave Prohibitions.

This program of koan study (*shitsunai shirabe*, literally, "in-the-room investigation") provides us with something like an elaborate tool kit for the ongoing inner work involved in Zen practice. The practitioner is thus invited to take a path forged through centuries by countless individuals who have traversed the same road before, with each koan as a new pointer along the way. In taking up this invitation, the practitioner ventures on a fascinating journey inwards, scaling the depths and breadth and heights of that infinite realm that is one's own true Self, continually finding new treasures and precious gems each step along the way.

This program of koan study involves repeated and frequent one-on-one encounters with the teacher, who has also gone through the process with a teacher, over a period of many years. It thus forges a bonding between teacher and student, an auspicious karmic connection of such depth and breadth that can never be adequately put into words.

The end result, if one can talk about results here, is that it enables practitioners to come back full circle and reclaim their full humanity, with a renewed sense of acceptance of their gifts and strengths as well as their shortcomings and weaknesses. They are able to see things more clearly with equanimity, and find peace within themselves. They are able to embrace the world, with all its pains and sufferings, as well as joys and hopes, and offer themselves, with hearts of compassion, to the world of sentient beings, to help in the healing of its wounds, with their unique gifts and talents and interests, from each of their particular stations in life. The three fruits of Zen, in other words, are about becoming truly human.

It is about smelling the aroma of coffee while sipping it from a cup in the morning, getting up and taking a walk, smelling the flowers, patting a dog as it wags its tail in glee, greeting a stranger along the way. It is also about getting tired after a hard day's work, feeling pain at a muscle strain, being indignant at the way the world is being run by so-called leaders, writing a letter to political representatives on an issue of concern. It is about getting sick, growing old, and, eventually, dying. But through all this, at each turn, in each and every encounter, you are fully there, tasting it fully. As you go along this path, you will continue to deepen your appreciation for all that is there, given, in this precious yet fragile condition of being human. One thousand blessings, ten thousand blessings. Gratitude, only gratitude.

The various items in this collection of Miscellaneous Koans present a sampling of the gems that await the practitioner in that journey inward, toward becoming fully and truly human. Zen Master Sister Elaine MacInnes has given the world a great gift in presenting her comments on these koans in published form. There are now a good number of books available in English by different Zen Masters with their commentaries on the main koan collections, such as the Gateless Gate, the Blue Cliff Record, the Book of Equanimity, and such—but this book of Sister Elaine's is the only one so far that takes up these Miscellaneous Koans, a small but very important collection that can play a crucial part in a practitioner's training.

Persons in the early stages of the Zen path will find in her words helpful guides for the journey. Practitioners who are well into the path will find fresh insights into these koans, and also recognize themes that they may already be familiar with from their own experience. Readers who are not yet practitioners may find here enough enticements to want to try this practice of Zen meditation for themselves. May it inspire you to accept this invitation, perhaps locate a practice center near you, check it out, and start sitting.

Come, taste and see!

Ruben L.F. Habito
Keiun-ken (Grace Cloud)
Maria Kannon Zen Center
Dallas, Texas

Preface

I have a strong suspicion that the decision to publish this book was occasioned by my being an octogenarian. These teisho were first given almost thirty years ago, as I was taking my first group of disciples through the gateless gate.

Subsequent sitters used them, starting a small groundswell. In any case, the impetus to publish came from the Toronto Zendo's Patrick Gallagher. His generous and steady hand has kept my manuscript reviewing and revision on course.

The obvious starting point, the teisho on the Miscellaneous Koans, was the first to receive attention. Next, my dear friend and mentor, Dr. Ruben Habito, Roshi of the Dallas Sanbo Kyodan Zendo, also a backer of this publishing plan, graciously agreed to write a foreword explaining something of the *kensho* (awakening or enlightenment) experience, and how the experience is deepened and matured in dokusan-room encounters, the private meetings between teacher and student. Thank you, Ben.

In May 2006, Patrick handed me the complete manuscript to check one last time, and, to my surprise, it included the three important koans worked on before the Miscellaneous Koans collection, and used by teachers in the Sanbo Kyodan tradition to bring their disciples through the satori experience. They are the Three Jewels: *Muji* (Mu, or Joshu's Dog); *Kongen* (The Root Source of Mu); and *Sekishu* (The Sound of One Hand).

Suddenly I was not so enthusiastic about offering all this to public scrutiny. Realizing there must be hundreds of teisho written on Joshu's

Dog, I was not too keen to add to that adequacy. The third koan, Sekishu, gave me pause to reconsider because it is rarely presented in teisho form, and most teachers leave it happily reposing in the confines of Hekigan-roku #18 (case 18 of the Blue Cliff Record). But I happen to feel keenly that at this point in history we very much need the teachings in The Sound of One Hand. Long discussions with my philosopher friend and mentor, Dr. Ernest McCullough, helped me reconstruct that teisho, and I became less averse to publishing it in this collection.

But it is concerning the second koan, Kongen, The Root Source of Mu, that I have the deepest reservations. I worked on that koan for many years in the dokusan room. During the eight years with Fukagai Roshi at Enkoji in Kyoto, I had no other koan. When I was transferred to the Sanbo Kyodan, Yamada Koun Roshi soon brought me to the point where I was able to "see" Mu clearly, and then the breakthrough with its Root Source was immediate and bright. My whole spiritual adventure seems to be written in that teisho, so it is an intimate revelation that I cherish. My chief hesitation is that one of the senior students at Yamada Roshi's Zendo in Kamakura warned me that nobody ever writes a teisho on Kongen, the Root Source of Mu.

I pass all these words—and remember, they are only words—to present and future sitters as they immerse themselves in the Great Matter, and find, to their delight, that indeed heaven starts right here, right now.

Sometimes I seem to give the lie to Meister Eckhart, who said that gratitude can be adequately expressed by one heart-felt and deep "thank you." Just one. Well, just one won't do here. I think first of those early sitters in the Manila Zendo, with only myself trying to be both teacher and role model. When some of them started to come to kensho, I assisted them through the first koans in the post-kensho period, by writing teisho on Joshu's Dog, The Source of Mu, and The Sound of One Hand, followed by the twenty-two koans collated by Harada Roshi, and part of the *Sanbo Kyodan's Book of Miscellaneous Koans*. In the ensuing years, there were two or three revisions as I traveled from Manila to Oxford, England, and to Toronto, Canada.

I thank my dear friend and mentor Dr. Ruben Habito Roshi of the Dallas Texas Zendo who, over the years, has been only a telephone call away to share his erudition and expertise in many areas. Ruben has written for this book a complete and stunning introduction to this early part of Zen training, which has elevated the text to new heights! Sometime in 2006, he and Patrick Gallagher, my editor in Toronto, decided to see if this portion of my writings could be made ready for publication. Patrick has been the kind of editor most writers long for. He made many trips to the convent as we cogitated changes or deletions, and helped to prime the flow when the waters in the well ran dry. Patrick and I both thank Josh Bartok of Wisdom Publications for his patience and polish.

I am grateful to all my teachers, my parents and religious community, the late Yamada Koun Roshi and Father Enomiya Lassalle, S.J. I acknowledge the myriad conveyors of wisdom in the whole creation family, toward a life of connection and reciprocity...hearing the "unhearable" in the roar of the Atlantic Ocean and to the Brahms recordings of Glenn Gould, and from the sightings of the "unseeable," in the empty silence of meditation.

What does one say nearing the end of a long life of rich experience? Looking back over eighty years, "naming the peaks" came to mind. And then I remembered the koan contained in this very text, "Which is higher, Mount Fuji or Mount Everest?" Before the disciple utters the obvious reply, the teacher whispers, "Only a fool would say 'Mount Everest!'"

And so perhaps Meister Eckhart's intuition prevails and one deep and broad "thank you" does penetrate the whole of creation, the sun and the moon and the stars. There remains only to acknowledge eternal gratitude to the consummate Source of this life and light and love.

Elaine MacInnes
Toronto, Ontario

Part One

The Three Jewels

Joshu's Dog

1

MUMON'S COMMENTARY

For the practice of Zen, you must pass the barrier set up by the ancient masters of Zen. To attain marvelous enlightenment, you must completely extinguish all the delusive thoughts of the ordinary mind. If you have not passed the barrier and have not extinguished delusive thoughts, you are a phantom haunting the weeds and trees. Now, just tell me, what is the barrier set up by the Zen masters of old? Merely this: Mu—the one barrier of our sect. It has come to be called "The Gateless Barrier of the Zen Sect."

Those who have passed the barrier are able not only to see Joshu face to face, but also walk hand in hand with the whole descending line of Zen masters and be eyebrow to eyebrow with them. You will see with the same eye they see with, hear with the same ear they hear with.

Wouldn't that be a wonderful joy? Is there anyone who doesn't want to pass this barrier? Then concentrate your whole self, with its 360 bones and joints and 84,000 pores, into Mu, making your whole body a solid lump of doubt. Day and night, without ceasing, keep digging into it, but don't take it as "nothingness" or as "being" or "non-being." It must be like a red-hot iron ball that you have gulped down and that you try to vomit up, but cannot. You must extinguish all delusive thoughts and feelings that you have cherished up to the present. After a certain period of such efforts, Mu will come to fruition, and inside and out will become one naturally. You will then be like a dumb person who has had a dream. You will know yourself, but for yourself only.

Then all of a sudden, Mu will break open and astonish the heavens and shake the earth. It will be just as if you had snatched the great sword of General Kan. If you meet a Buddha, you will kill him. If you meet an ancient Zen master, you will kill him. Though you may stand on the brink of life and death, you will enjoy the great freedom. In the six realms and the four modes of birth, you will live in the samadhi of innocent play.

Now, how should you concentrate on Mu? Exhaust every ounce of energy you have in doing it. And if you do not give up on the way, you will be enlightened the way a candle in front of the Buddha is lit by one touch of fire.

THE VERSE

Dog! Buddha Nature!
The perfect manifestation, the absolute command;
A little "has" or "has not"
And the body is lost! Life is lost!

TEISHO ON THE CASE

The case is very concise. The koan involves two people only, a monk and his teacher. We are not told anything more about the monk except that he is a monk. He could be a very green monk; he could be a half-done monk; he could be well on toward becoming ripe. But let's suppose he was like the people in our zendo who are working on Mu, people who are usually rather new to Zen. The monk had doubtless read many of the sutras, and he had probably, to some degree or other, become convinced of and enamored by this beautiful Inner Life, the essence of all creation that Shakyamuni spoke about following his great enlightenment. And perhaps, while reflecting on this wonderful Essential Nature, he happened to see a dog, a dreadful-looking dog, running across the temple floor. So he started to wonder: "Can that miserable looking dog have this beautiful Essential Nature that Lord Buddha told us about?" His wonderment obviously led to doubt. Finally, he did what a good student should do: he took his doubts to his teacher. And we must also not overlook the other possibility that the monk was, even at that point, asking Joshu to show him the real Buddha Nature, and was not asking for its *interpretation* or meaning at all.

The teacher is a truly great Zen master—Joshu, who lived from 778 to 897. He had his first *satori* (enlightenment experience) when he was eighteen years old. He went to Nansen to study at an early age and opened their long relationship with a now-famous encounter. When Joshu first arrived at Nansen's, the Master was sick in bed. He asked Joshu, "Where have you come from?" Joshu replied, "I have come from the place of the Auspicious Image." "Did you see the Auspicious Image?" Nansen asked. "No," replied Joshu, "but I have seen a reclining Tathagata."

After this promising beginning, Joshu stayed under Nansen for forty years as a disciple, until Nansen's death. Joshu was then fifty-eight years old. Following the custom of the times, he went on a pilgrimage visiting different Zen masters to engage in "Dharma combat" to sharpen his insight. Finally, when he was eighty, he allowed himself to be approached by students and settled down as a teacher in a place called Joshu, from where he got his name.

Dogen Zenji, like most Zen masters, never handed out bouquets—but he did admire Joshu and called him the old Buddha. Joshu is also famous for the rules he wrote for monastic observance, and I understand that the contemporary monastic schedule is still based on Joshu's guidelines. They are the legacy of a very great Zen master indeed.

Now I'd like to say something about the temperament of this Zen Master Joshu. In so many of our koans, the master is a kind of bumptious person. Perhaps Rinzai comes to mind first—General Rinzai with his dynamically sharp spirit and thunderous cry, *"Katsu!"* Or there is Bokushu who, as soon as a student entered the dokusan room, would grab him roughly by the collar and shout, "Say it!" There was Unmon, who was very famous for the strict and severe way he guided his disciples.

But Joshu wasn't like that. In fact, they say his ordinary speaking voice was soft and low, not much more than a gentle whisper. His Zen was quiet, as was that of Dogen Zenji and Shakyamuni. When the monk asked him if the dog had Buddha Nature or not, Joshu probably gently replied, "Mu."

I am reminded of an incident I saw in Japan some years ago. I was in *sesshin* (meditation retreat) at Takatsuki in Kansai, and one day Yamada Roshi's assistant changed the room where we went to write after dokusan. That evening after dokusan, I entered this room and sat down and began to write. I heard a very loud voice, which was indeed a shout, calling out *"Muji ni sanjite orimasu!"* ("I am working on Mu!") I looked up, and a short distance away at a kind of angle was the doku-san room; there beside the open window was Yamada Roshi. In front of him was a disciple. The Roshi was rubbing his face and eyes in that vigorous way he did when he was tired, and the disciple, who was obviously in desperation shouted again, *"Sanjite orimasu!"* The Roshi finished his massaging, took his hands away from his face, looked at the disciple directly and kindly, and said very gently, "What did you say?"

Now about this word *Mu.* One student working on Mu said recently that he is a little disturbed by Mu because he knows it is a negation, that it means "No." I should like to point out that there is another koan: "A monk asked Joshu, 'Does a dog have Buddha Nature or not?' Joshu answered, 'U.'"—which is positive. In Case 30 of the Gateless Gate, Taibai asked Baso in earnestness, "What is Buddha?" Baso answered, "The very mind is Buddha." And then in Case 33, a monk asked Baso in all earnestness, "What is Buddha?" Baso replied, "No mind, no Buddha." Whether it's yes or no, mind or not-mind, it doesn't make any difference. So don't give any thought to yes or no. Don't give any thought to anything.

I think we are very fortunate that when studying this koan in English we simply leave it as Mu and do not translate it as "no" or "not" or "not-being." In English, Mu is harmless. It is just something a cow says and has little appeal to the intellect. It is relatively easy to stop thinking about Mu. (Though there might be a problem for those well-versed in Greek and contemporary physics. In that language, we are told there is hidden a whole world of Mu. In one case, the Greek letter Mu symbolizes the coefficient of friction and is used as a symbol in thermodynamics and electromagnetism. But I'm sure we sitters can discard the Greek approach to Mu with no difficulty at all.)

Remember, for most of us our intellect is overworked. It's a wonderful faculty, but just because it's wonderful doesn't mean we have to use it for all occasions. I am reminded of a story told by Bishop Tudtud from Mindanao in the southern Philippines. He said one of their seminarians had been ordained a deacon just before Christmas. The bishop gave him a watch to mark the occasion. He asked the new deacon to preach at Midnight Mass, and the young priest-to-be told the congregation four times during the sermon what time it was! How wonderful a watch is for telling time! In another area our intellect is wonderful, too, and it helps us in so many of our problems and enterprises. It is unsurpassed at analyzing and investigating and breaking down complexities. But when we are trying to meet Reality, or what Yamada Roshi calls the Empty-Infinite, the intellect is useless because we can't break *IT* down.

Now let us take another look at the question in this koan. When a monk or any Zen disciple asks a teacher if a dog has Buddha Nature or not, the answer has to be "yes," "no," or "maybe." And these are all intellectual answers. When a student asks a Zen master an intellectual question, it's the business of the teacher to get the repartee out of the field of intellectual responses, the field of "yes," "no," and "maybe." A good teacher would never answer like that. Those answers feed the very faculty that it is their business to stop functioning. That's the appropriateness of Mu in English. It's not very nourishing intellectually.

Mu is a wonderful broom to sweep away all the thoughts and ideas and concepts that keep the intellect fed and working. That's its proper activity, to sweep and to empty. When people come to dokusan right after *shoken* (formally becoming a student) they usually have a lot to say. This is an easy time for a roshi, and interesting too, because we hear all kinds of stories about dogs and Buddhas and monks and temples and such things. But after the Mu has been sweeping for a while, these stories gradually come to an end. To the teacher, this speechlessness of the student is a good sign. When all words are exhausted and there is nothing to say, then the teacher takes the initiative.

After one's sitting deepens, something happens to Mu, and in teaching we use it as a handle. It is the subject of what is called *mondo*, repartee. The thrusts of mondo are best when they arise from silence. Together, teacher and disciples will investigate Mu, its rises and falls.

This stage of becoming intimate with Mu is the stage of building *joriki,* the power that arises from sitting. The kanji for *jo* means "to be settled or quiet," and has overtones of foundation; *riki* is power. Lao Tzu tells us that silence is the great revelation. As silence deepens, we experience change, and we discover to our delight that revelation is not knowledge; revelation is power, a power that brings transformation and insight and, as you may have noticed, in the mondo at the beginning of the teisho, the time and place are always here and now.

TEISHO ON MUMON'S COMMENTARY

Let us now look at Mumon's commentary. Mumon himself came to the second stage of Zen practice, satori, after working on Mu for six years. This commentary is his *kensho-ki* (a written account of the kensho experience). He says, *"For the practice of Zen, you must pass the barrier set up by the ancient masters of Zen."* The barrier is the koan Mu. *"To attain marvelous enlightenment, you must completely extinguish all the delusive thoughts of the ordinary mind."* As long as you are using the intellect, you will not come to know intuitively. *"If you have not passed the barrier and have not extinguished delusive thoughts, you are a phantom haunting the weeds and trees."* Those are the bad names he is throwing out at Muji people (i.e., people working on Mu): you are phantoms, haunting weeds and trees! You are *wak-wak* (a ghost), as they say in Leyte. *"Now, just tell me, what is the barrier set up by the Zen masters of old? Merely this: Mu—the one barrier of our sect."* Muji (the written character of "mu") is true Soto, but many Rinzai temples now also use this koan for pre-kensho study. *"It has come to be called 'The Gateless Barrier of the Zen Sect.'"* Yamada Roshi called his book on the Mumonkan *The Gateless Gate* because in the end, when you pass the gate, you discover there never was any gate there to begin with.

"Those who have passed the barrier are able not only to see Joshu face to face, but also to walk hand in hand with the whole descending line of Zen masters and be eyebrow to eyebrow with them." These are all the delightful people spoken of in the koans and teisho and it's not that you're so close that your eyebrow is pressed against their eyebrow! That expression is about as close as words can get to express Oneness. One with Joshu himself, and Shakyamuni and Unmon and Dogen Zenji and Harada Roshi and Yamada Roshi!

"You will see with the same eye they see with, hear with the same ear they hear with. Wouldn't that be a wonderful joy?...Then concentrate your whole self, with its 360 bones and joints and 84,000 pores, into Mu, making your whole body a solid lump of doubt." I'd like to make a little observation here. Mumon lived almost five hundred years after Joshu. Now a few minutes ago we spoke about Joshu and his gentle spirit. We saw him coaxing his disciple out of the world of duality into Oneness by the gentle "peck" of Mu. We just can't imagine him thundering to get 84,000 pores into a great lump of doubt. Here we have two different personalities five hundred years apart. Time brings changes in pedagogy in all fields. In our lifetime, right in the Sanbo Kyodan, our stream of Zen, we have seen quite a bit of change. Yasutani Roshi was still alive when I first started to attend their *zazenkai* (day-long retreats),

and he, like his teacher, Harada Roshi, ran a rather lively zendo during sesshin. Both of those teachers allowed one day of sesshin "open" to sound—that is, everyone working on Mu could say it out as loud as they wanted to. Can you imagine a more aggravating basis for sitting than being in a room all day with fifty people all pressing audibly on their practice! And not only that, there were usually four *godo* (well-seasoned students in charge of discipline), all brandishing a *kyosaku* (awakening stick) with great flourish—and not limited to two strokes on each shoulder! Accounts in *The Three Pillars of Zen* tell us that many sitters became exhausted and nervous just hearing other people being hit!

Yamada Roshi changed all that. It may be partly due to his temperament, but Yamada Roshi felt that Dogen Zenji and Joshu and Shakyamuni all fostered quiet Zen. And he had acquired a lot of experience in working with people from many countries all over the world. I well remember one North American saying, "I will not be hit into kensho!"

All this leads me to believe that we do not have to take Mumon's advice literally. Not only that, but I strongly advise you not to. I don't want anyone coming into the dokusan room to me with a built-up solid lump of doubt. I'm not saying that nothing will happen when you do Mu. Mu is abrasive and, sincerely done, will produce results. Something will happen. That is why a teacher is necessary, as guide during that descent to the depths of self. But I want to see that you go at a speed you can handle. This is another reason that Muji people should come to dokusan regularly, even if you have nothing to say. Remember, a blank consciousness is the best condition.

In the commentary on this koan, Mumon relates how he came to kensho. He says, *"Day and night, without ceasing, keep digging into it, but don't take it as 'nothingness' or as 'being' or 'non-being.'"* It must be like a red-hot iron ball that you have gulped down, which is that "leap in the dark," referring to the moment when we have to "let go" and "leap." Unconsciously, some people resist. *"You must extinguish all delusive thoughts and feelings that you have cherished up to the present."* He goes on to say, *"After a certain period of such efforts, Mu will come to fruition, and inside and out will become one naturally."* You meet non-duality.

Here I follow Shibayama Roshi in inserting the sentence that appears a little later. *"Then all of a sudden, Mu will break open and astonish the heavens and shake the earth."* When will this happen, you ask? Yamada Roshi says it will happen when all things are ready, to which Dogen

Zenji would add—and a touch of help comes from beyond. Some people refer to their kensho as a mountain that in time may seem like a pimple on a great plain. But at the time, it is a Mount Fuji or Mount Mayon.

"You will then be like a dumb person who has had a dream. You will know yourself, but for yourself only." The experience is essentially incommunicable. Even if you have considerable skill with words, you will not be able to relate the experience satisfactorily. You will, however, be able to speak of it relatively. You will be intimate with many of the words and phrases we use in dokusan and teisho. That is one of the advantages of hearing frequent teisho.

Sometimes the opening experience is not very forceful. Sitters usually have preconceived ideas about kensho, and unless the "happening" meets their expectations, they do not confirm themselves, so to speak. Confirmation of kensho is the teacher's business. Leave that to her or him. The emptying in your sitting should get rid of the delusion of kensho or not. In our stream of Zen, the confirmation of kensho is dependent on answers to a prescribed set of questions. Of course, it goes without saying that there are other factors, and I will always help the person who has had an experience to come to some understanding of what happened. But that is the business of being a teacher. Your business, as Mumon says, is to concentrate on Mu and to use up your energy doing it. All of this is just on the periphery, however. The experience itself is incommunicable.

Mumon goes on to talk about the effects of the experience. *"It will be just as if you had snatched the great sword of General Kan. If you meet a Buddha, you will kill him. If you meet an ancient Zen master, you will kill him."* Notice they are *ancient* Zen masters—not extant ones!

These are all ideas. In sitting, things in the head have to be gotten rid of. Kensho is an experience quite apart from all this; and when it happens you are well aware of the fact. At least for a time after kensho, people are very sure of themselves. It is quite delightful, really. There's usually not a doubt, and an argument with Buddha would ensue if he came along and said something contrary to the experience.

"Though you may stand on the brink of life and death, you will enjoy the great freedom. In the six realms and the four modes of birth, you will live in the samadhi of innocent play."

"Now, how should you concentrate on Mu? Exhaust every ounce of energy you have in doing it." As I said above, we give that advice with

qualifications. *"And if you do not give up on the way, you will be enlightened the way a candle in front of the Buddha is lit by one touch of fire."* If you persevere, as surely as the coming of dawn or the rain of early spring—BANG!—the bottom of the barrel will disappear! As quick as a flash of lightning!

That is Mumon's story as he tells of his own six-year practice, and his ensuing enlightenment.

TEISHO ON THE VERSE

Dog! Buddha Nature!
The perfect manifestation, the absolute command;
A little "has" or "has not"
And body is lost! Life is lost!

"A little 'has' or 'has not'" is the concept of discrimination. Sitters who are this far along in their practice know that insight and freedom are not attained in the world of having or not having. Look at what is being presented by Joshu. There is no debate or complexity about the dog, or the Buddha Nature, or commanding and manifesting. They are simply dog, Buddha Nature, commanding, manifesting. We are being told, that "a little" discrimination throws the whole Zen world out of whack. That shows how destructive mental and intellectual procedures can be to our sitting. Even a little, even a little.

We frequently come across that phrase, "a little," in our Zen studies, and eventually we come to understand that it has an absolute meaning. It absolutely says that there must be no intellection at all. This is rather difficult to swallow and can almost seem devastating when we have spent most of the waking hours during our life intellectualizing. And even into old age, when it seems that Zen meditators carry on with their work, there is a certain proclivity to approaching the next minute through the intellectual door.

So I want to say a word of encouragement to all. If you find yourself in the area of the dualistic world, not totally but rather "somewhat," then don't give up. Godos in our zendos frequently shout *"Gambatte!"* which means "persevere," "stick to it." In the verse of Case 39 in the Mumonkan we read, "Angling in a swift stream, those greedy for bait will be caught. If you open your mouth even a little bit, your life will be lost."

John of the Cross tells us that there is often just a thin thread holding back a bird from flying where it will, but it might as well be a steel cable! Sometimes, it is just a little bit of delusion that keeps us from being free. It so often means that we have only a little bit further to go to have true insight.

So be encouraged, especially if you are aware of this "little bit." Perhaps with just a little bit more sitting, a little bit of deepening, that little bit of duality will be swept away. I don't know if this is of any comfort to you, but Yamada Roshi used to counsel us to remember that when we are tired and discouraged, even a little bit, the "enemy" is also tired and discouraged, even a little bit.

It is important that meditators feel that as they advance in Zen they will not necessarily become great strong leaders. Perhaps they will, if they have the innate potential. But you will be who you were meant to be, which is the peace and comfort of the satori experience. So if you feel you are just an ordinary person, then that is the most appropriate, and consequently you may be the one to allow things to happen and unfold, when dust storms arise. The great South American teacher Paolo Freire used to tell his followers that the humanization of the world cannot be accomplished by the strong and powerful. He'd say it is going to be the little ones, the unarmed and the not powerful, who, when healed, will have the freedom to release the liberating spirit. Orthopedic doctors tell a similar tale about a broken body bone. Once it is set and healed, it is stronger than the original bone, and its greatest strength is the very point of the break itself.

So if we get discouraged sometimes with the "little" lingering delusion on the road to liberation, let us remember that the seeping away of the delusion, the healing of it, will be, in time, our greatest strength. Only then can we as individuals do something truly constructive about the social injustices in our world. Until we are free, we don't have much to give others, except further delusion.

What is Kongen, *the origin of Mu?*

2

Kongen is a kind of double-barrel word, which means both "root" and "source." Together they suggest the ultimate or root-source. So in English the koan could read, "What is the root-source of Mu?"

Because it comes right after the magnificent Muji koan, Kongen is especially profound. In the Sambo Kyodan, our stream of Zen, this one is almost not a koan. The Rinzai school treats it a little differently, and reaches a certain level, a level we also touch. But the Soto school takes it beyond that point. Unless you take it beyond and beyond, until it blows the mind, you have never tasted the koan nor allowed it to enrich you. Your contemplation, your spirituality, will not have true depth until you have experienced the root-source of Mu, until that root-source becomes the fabric of your Zen. As long as you find God reasonable and comprehensible and knowable, you are in touch with the eschatological and transcendent God only. The horizontal—the immanent God—is the way of Mu. To paraphrase Father Raimundo Panikkar, it is the other side of God's face that is shown to the Orient.

When you find Mu, you will easily discover its root. But what is the source of that root? Confucius has said, "To know what you know and what you don't know is the characteristic of one who knows." Having come to the knowing of the root, one comes to the not-knowing of the source.

Ultimately, there is a mystery at the core of the Void. In Zen, we must be careful of referring to mystery. Yamada Roshi says there is no mystery but the *fact* itself. This koan, however, is the one exception. It is also, among all the koans, the one most overtly religious. If a teacher were a trained theologian, this teisho could be called, "A theology for the Oriental contemplative." John of the Cross defines contemplation as the silencing or emptying of our sense and spiritual faculties. All our theological knowledge from this koan can be learned only by emptying our mind and senses.

As said above, ultimately there is a mystery at the core of the Void. *Muji no Kongen* is an invitation to that core. As Lao Tzu says in the Tao Te Ching, "Impenetrable is the darkness where the heart of Being dwells. From eternity to eternity It will never perish. Who saw the beginning of All?" Or to quote another ancient Chinese sage, Wang Wei (699–759):

> *When there is nothing to give up,*
> *One has indeed reached the source.*
> *When there is no void to abide in,*
> *One is indeed experiencing the void,*
> *Transcending quiescence is no action;*
> *Rather, it is Creation, which constantly acts.*

Once the third eye has been opened, no matter how tentatively, we must reach for Kongen. Although the world's beginning may naturally be considered, this is not a question of past and future. Kongen and nirvana are here, now. All of creation, whatever exists, is silently concentrated right here, right now—in my own creation, in my own being. Likewise, all of creation is a beginning and is pervaded by what I myself am. The beginning and nirvana are upon us. But if we seem apparently lost and wandering and seeking, we are already encompassed by infinite blessedness. As Mumon says so beautifully in the verse to Case 35 in the Gateless Gate, "All are blessed, ten thousand things, ten thousand blessings." Original Blessing indeed!

I propose that this approach is the Asian soul. Everything we learn from the root of Mu tells us we come from Original Blessing. And when the Federation of Asian Bishops' Conference (India, 1978) stated, "The techniques developed in Asian religious traditions, for example, Yoga and Zen, are of great service to the prayer experience of immanence. The spirituality of immanence can lead us to newer insights into theology." I wonder if the root doesn't tell us that the newer insights are older insights after all. Long before original sin became the start of the Church's theology, the Asian sages had a deep, innate, positive, blessing-filled religious sense.

The Asian bishops went on to say that Asian Christians are to have an Asian spirituality. The root of Mu tells us this has to be based on Original Blessing. By then a further step is revealed, and in the ancients' unrelenting search and hunger for God, and their patient acceptance of the void in deep meditation and silence, they came to its source. Having come to the knowing of the root, they prostrated themselves before the non-knowing of the source.

Rinzai is root, and Soto is root-source. In root, we find we are of God. In root-source, we discover our limitation. And this experience has nothing to do with an elitist consciousness. Both Rinzai and Soto teach that we decline pronouncements on things we can never really know "in this world"; for instance, things before birth and after death. Let us keep within the limits of our experience. Kongen has a built-in curb to our morbid curiosity.

Kongen is the unutterable inconceivability of God.

Lao Tzu again:

> *The Tao that can be told of*
> *is not the Absolute Tao;*
> *The names that can be given*
> *are not the Absolute Names.*

If God is utterly inconceivable, then ultimately so am I. "Therefore I ask God to rid me of God. The nonbeing Being of God is beyond God, beyond all differentiation; there was I alone, wanting myself alone, and saw myself as the one who had made this man [this woman or myself]! So I am the cause of myself and of all things. But if I were not, God were not." Aren't those the words of Meister Eckhart? Let us not slip up on the words (as Unmon tells the monk in Case 39 of the Gateless Gate).

In Zen there is a saying, "The truth that is as it is, has been continuous since antiquity, without ever having varied so much as a hair's breadth." Kongen is the family treasure. It does not come in through the gate. In the preface to his book, Mumon says: "Zen makes no-gate the gate of Dharma."

It is no-gate from the start. How can we pass through it? Haven't you heard the old saying, "Things that come in through the gate are not the family treasure!" Such remarks are just like raising heavy waves when there is no wind, or gouging a wound in healthy skin. How much more ridiculous to adhere to words and phrases or try to understand by means of the intellect. It is exactly like trying to strike the moon with a stick, or to scratch an itchy foot through the sole of your boot.

The mystery of the root-source of Mu is the contemplative's school. It can also be the point where the theologian becomes contemplative. The following is from the writing of the eminent theologian of the twentieth century, Karl Rahner. He seems to speak of the origin of Mu.

> Our beginning is hidden in God. It is decided. Only when we have arrived will we fully know what our origin is. For God is mystery as such, and what he posited when he established us in our beginning is still the mystery. Without evacuating the mystery, we can say that there belongs to our beginning all that is there, everything whatsoever which exists, and is silently concentrated in the wellspring of our own existence. And is pervaded by what each is in himself, and herself, posited by God as a beginning uniquely and unrepeatedly. With what is hard and what is easy, delicate and harsh, with what belongs to the abyss and what is heavenly. All is encompassed by God's knowledge and love. All has to be accepted.... The possibility of acceptance itself belongs to the might of the divinely posited beginning. And if we accept, we have accepted sheer love and happiness. And the more that love and forgiveness which encompasses and belongs to our beginning is accepted in the pain of life, and in the death which gives life, the more this original element emerges and manifests itself and pervades our history.... When the beginning has found itself in the fulfillment and has been fulfilled in the freedom of accepting love, GOD WILL BE ALL IN ALL.

So speaks an eminent theologian. Our final arrival is mystery and so is our root-source; to face our infinite incomprehensibility is to be a contemplative.

We meditators not only face the infinite incomprehensibility of the Infinite, but also our own hiddenness. And when contemplation is born, all objects die. Where God is concerned, contemplation is appropriate, for God is utterly unknowable by reason, and no thought can give us an idea of what he is.

The medieval Saint Richard of St. Victor says, "Contemplatives who endeavor to think, only kill their incipient mystical life...they are like mothers who strangle their children at birth." He continues, "Let them be quiet, still, expectant, calm, lest they smother the tiny flame which is their most precious possession." And so he goes on that all thoughts, all desires and hopes, all fears, all images and all ambitions—all must be trampled down under the cloud of forgetting. His "forget, forget, forget" is like the *"nada, nada, nada"* of John of the Cross. And it is the most natural thing in the world, to compare these texts with the Zen Masters: "Empty, empty, empty" "Mu, Mu, Mu." Where there is nothing, there is everything. What is the root-source of nothing?

In our Zen stream spirituality, we seek the return of our Original Nature to its original spontaneity. For a while, perhaps when we begin, we see this Original Nature as an object. But soon we have to give up the attempt to make our nature an object of contemplation. We have to eliminate all symbols and all thoughts, and *allow this nature to be totally itself, pure and spontaneous.* You will remember being told in the first couple of years of sitting, "There is still a gap between you and Mu." The closing of this gap is kensho, when we "see" in a flash. But enlightenment was not always seen this way.

The origin of *dhyana* (the Sanskrit word for meditation which comes down to us as *zen*) is lost in history. Its root is found in the Vedic Books of India, completed by 1500 B.C. We know from our koan study that the Indians taught fifty-two steps to enlightenment. We read in some books that it was based on a process that caused the disciple to pass through a series of stages of progressive simplification of thought and an increasing sublimation of the "object" of contemplation. Obviously, enlightenment came when thought was simplified to nothing at all, and the object of contemplation was sublimated out of existence. For many people this could be a natural process.

Our friend, the late Father Yves Raguin, S.J., has clearly outlined the history of our Mu and the changes it underwent in China. The teaching of Bodhidharma, who was the first Zen ancestor in China, is contained in the Lankavatara Sutra. He taught a method of total concentration in order to free the mind from all false notions and all attachments. The fruit of his efforts was to be a revelation of the purity of the Original Nature. As Father Raguin says:

The main idea of this scripture is that the true state of nirvana is total emptiness devoid of any characteristics, duality, or differentiation. It is inexpressible in words and inconceivable in thought. *Our emancipation consists in our intuition of this highest truth.* Every human being is capable of this because everyone has the Buddha Nature. But our minds are obscured by desires, erroneous thoughts, and attachments of all sorts. Therefore, Bodhidharma taught the method of undisturbed concentration as if one faced a wall (hence the legend of the nine-year meditation) to free the mind from erroneous thoughts and attachments. Eventually the mind must become free from everything even to the extent of abandoning both being and nonbeing. Bodhidharma also taught ascetic practices in order to reassert our originally pure nature.

Six generations after Bodhidharma, Zen in China became divided into the Northern and Southern Schools. The Sandokai ("Identity of Phenomena and Essential"), which we chant at Vespers, makes mention of the Northern and Southern Patriarch. The founders of both schools, Shen-hsui in the North and Hui-neng (Eno) in the South, originally had the same teacher, Hung-jen.

The Northern School was seen at the time as holding tradition, which D.T. Suzuki epitomized by their acceptance that "the seen and the seeing are two separate entities." The Southern School united these entities, and called it *chien-hsieng* (*kensho* in Japanese). To see the ultimate reality of all things, the original nature. It is no longer a matter of thought as intermediary to reality. There exists only one thing, one single reality, and since it is not separate, there are no stages to go through. The awakening to the reality of the Original Nature can only be sudden, for there is no possible intermediary.

In many ways, we can say Mu entered the Way at this point in history. The tag *Mu* was affixed to the Way in the Southern School of Zen in China (our lineage) and flourished. Its success was due to its radical nature. Historians tell us this marked a stage in the Sinocization of Buddhism. Eno, the Sixth Ancestor, assimilated something of the abrupt nature of Taoist contemplation by stressing the absolute spontaneity of the Original Nature. Taoism has instituted absence of thought as its doctrine. Absence of thought means not to be carried away by thought in the process of thought. But if one can cut all thought for one instant from all attachment to what exists, then the Original Nature is freed to act spontaneously and appropriately.

The Orient would have its beginning in the darkness of blessing, and freeing our Original Nature. Therefore, our journey is letting go and letting Be-ing be! This is our contemplation. As said before, when contemplation is born, all objects die, and we let them die. Where there is nothing, there is everything. We cannot find the root-source of nothing until we let go. We let go of the past. I am not alive if I cling to yesterday, because yesterday is just a memory. It's not real; it's a creation of the mind. To live in yesterday is to be dead. Let go of the past. Let us establish our own personal program of peace and reconciliation, and grant amnesty to all the people we resent and have grievances against. Let us free our prisoners. Let us also let go of our regrets, our losses and failures, our hang-ups and mistakes and handicaps, our bad luck and unfortunate experiences and lack of opportunities. We also have to let go of our successes and good experiences because they too become oppressive if they keep us dead in the past. We must continually say goodbye to people, occupations, things, and places that we have treasured in the past. We shall never meet again, because when we return we shall have changed. So: thank you and goodbye to the past.

Where there is nothing there is everything.

Let us also let go of our tomorrows, for, like the past, they are a construction of the mind. If we live in the future, we are dead to the present. Let us drop our desires and ambitions, which are our bondage to anxiety. "Creations are innumerable, I resolve to free them all." The root-source of nothing is Lao Tzu's "impenetrable is the darkness where the heart of Being dwells." And this is our other side of letting go, letting Be-ing be.

"I live now, not I, but Christ lives within me." The perfect communion of the saint and Absolute.

And all our exploring of the root-source of Mu is to arrive where we started and, as T.S. Eliot says, to know the place for the first time.

And meditation is not in time. Martin Buber tells us, rather, time is prayer. To reverse the relation is to abolish reality.

The koan of the root-source of Mu is a "journey-back" in time *and* space. It is an experiential journey of the utmost importance for a meditator. The presentation of this koan in the dokusan room must be unaligned wisdom. Our transformation must begin in the darkness and the letting-go and letting-be to the root-source of Mu.

These few words from "You Darkness," by Rainer Maria Rilke speak beautifully of the cosmic womb of our origin:

> *fire makes*
> *a circle of light*
> *darkness pulls in everything...*
> *powers and people—*
> *and it is possible a great energy*
> *is moving near me.*
> *I have faith in nights.*

And this seems the night that John of the Cross speaks of, the night that cleanses memory.

—with special thanks to two Jesuits, Karl Rahner and Yves Raguin

What is the Sound of One Hand?

3

TEISHO ON THE CASE

This is the third of the trilogy, one of the three deep koans. The first, Muji, Joshu's Dog, invites us to discover ourselves. The second, *Kongen*, the root-source of Mu, invites us to discover the Infinite. And the third, *Sekishu*, the Sound of One Hand, invites us to discover the universe. If Kongen is the non-being God, then Sekishu is the being God.

It is said that Hakuin used this as a koan, and it originates in Setcho's interpolation of Case 18 of the Hekiganroku, the Blue Cliff Record, "The Design of the National Teacher's Tomb." The koan goes something like this.

The Emperor Shukuso asked the National Teacher what kind of mausoleum he wanted erected after his death, and the teacher said he wanted a seamless tomb. When the Emperor asked about the design, the National Teacher gave a silent reply, which the Emperor couldn't understand. When the Emperor pressed for a meaning, the teacher said to ask his Dharma successor. So when the National Teacher died, the Emperor went to his Dharma successor, told him he meant to erect a monument for the deceased Zen master, and asked about the meaning of the teacher's former replies. The Dharma successor said, "From the south of the lake, to the north of river." And it is here that Setcho comments, "The single hand does not sound needlessly."

One memory of this koan goes back many years. Louise Behrend, my violin teacher at Juilliard, was giving a concert in Japan and said she wanted to meet a Zen master. I took her to Somon Horisawa, the colorful custodian of the beautiful Shakado Temple on Mount Hiei, overlooking Kyoto. A very spirited person, she settled herself on the zabuton in front of him. She suddenly lifted her hand and gave a very loud snap of the fingers before the monk. "That's the sound of one hand," she explained with great pleasure to the smiling Horisawa-san.

When I started to teach Zen in the Philippines, I was surprised at the number of people who had heard of this koan. Not only that, but several brave people said they thought they could answer "What is the sound of one hand?" I'd always invite them to a joust. "Show me the sound of one hand!" Almost always they would raise a hand, as my violin teacher did, and snap their fingers, smartly or timidly, according to the spirit. And I would lean over, look them straight in the eye, and say reverently, "I didn't hear anything at all." Only some got a message, but all knew the presentation wouldn't do. Yasutani Roshi used to say that everything that can be written in the head is not the *shin no jijitsu,* the heart of the fact.

Shibayama Roshi called this koan "Master Hakuin's own barrier." Hakuin Zenji saw this koan as a means of "waiting for a brave warrior, by setting a high price." It is widely used in Rinzai even yet, as a means of coming to kensho. This koan is especially intimate to me. I have worked with it three times and then another fifty-three times.

It was first given to me by Fukagai Roshi, at the Rinzai nuns' temple of Enkoji in the northern area of Kyoto. For seven or eight years, anytime I went to dokusan, I said only the word *sekishu.* I had no other koan. After I transferred to his sangha, the Sanbo Kyodan, Yamada Roshi took me through Muji and Kongen and then we went on to Sekishu. As you can imagine, after so many years of preparation, the world lit up for me, as I broke through that koan. "Form is empiness; emptiness is form." "Where there is nothing, the limitless storehouse." The sound of one hand is our original face. To which Ikkyu deftly replied, "Mr. Original Face cuts a fancy figure: one look and it's love at first sight."

The third time I "did" the koan was with Sister Angela Gutierrez, R.G.S. Sister was the second person to enter the Manila sangha, and she was our first to enter nirvana. Every day, for one-and-a-half years before her death, I visited her. The visits were a kind of dokusan. Five or six months before her death, she had a kensho experience and then proceeded to the Kongen koan, where for three days she plunged into its abyss, to her great awe and enrichment. Then she came to the Sekishu koan, and for a full week she wandered around the universe in great delight. It was like another kensho for both of us.

It happened that at the time I was reading Rahner, and she put his words into life:

> We must be growing always, as it were absorbing infinities into ourselves, because it is our business to remain open. And so life, our being, is full of endless potential that we explore only by degrees, step by step, piecemeal. If we keep enriching ourselves in this way, accumulating grace and blessings, ever more ego-less and faithful, absorbing the Infinite, then we begin to see the kind of love we can give away to others, simply by giving away ourselves.

With this koan, Angelita seemed to break out of her human unfreedom and for one week, step by step, first here and then there, she heard the sound of one hand with ever-increasing clarity.

And how do we see that universe, with all three eyes open? As one vast, all-embracing, all-distinguishing event. The self-communication of God. This activity creates the universe and its tremendous evolution. So the sound of one hand leads to celebration, as in each moment our hidden beginning finds fulfillment.

Angelita reminds us in her *kensho-ki* it is found in the singing of a cricket and the morning winds, the twittering of a nightingale, a mother's lullaby, a baby, a flower, a tree, a cloud. In her words, she realized the sound of one hand, "I saw with my ears, and heard with my heart, and understood with my eyes." And that is the essence of the Sound of One Hand.

Seeing with your ears, and hearing with your heart, and understanding with your eyes in the Zen mirrorlike mind, reflecting the universe just as it is—its totality, excluding nothing. It reflects all things in the universe in an equal way, just like a mirror. A mirror does not reflect only the beautiful and not the ugly, or only the colorful and not the drab, or only the rich and not the poor. It reflects everything, just as it is. It also reflects each thing in all its uniqueness, each thing being what it is uniquely. The mirrorlike enlightened mind is able to respond appropriately to whatever it reflects, or as St. Paul says, "To be all things to all men." To the hungry, food; to the naked, clothes. Just that.

Each day, Angelita's mirrorlike mind would reflect a particular thing and she could not take her eyes, her three eyes, from it, in total awe and wonder and delight. Each day seemed to hold a longer and deeper gaze. And then one day, she "saw" the host at communion. Truly, she was never the same. From that day on, "the sound of one hand" became a kind of password in dokusan. It represented the length and breadth and height and depth of the limits of Angelita's ability to touch the Infinite. It was a true koan for her. And in the words of Rahner, "Live in me, pray with me, suffer with me, more I do not ask."

This can be a true koan for us all. You can imagine the kind of tingle that goes through my whole being when someone comes to dokusan and says, "I am working on the sound of one hand." I usually say, "That sound can resound to the very limits of your capacity!" and I say a little prayer that it will.

Like all koans, this one has infinite depths. Sink yourself into it in becoming *ONE*. Then the "I" will disappear and you will find that only God is "I." I am the Thou that God utters. Here is a paraphrase of Abishiktananda (Dom Henri Le Saux, a French Benedictine monk who pioneered an integration of Hindu and Christian spirituality) from his book *Prayer*:

> The urgent need is that my encounter with "that man," in that very place, at that very moment, should bring out more brightly, the spontaneity of the Essential Nature, the image of God, should unveil his secret mystery, both in him and in me. It is really in such meetings, in the communion of man with each other, that the Infinite manifests and reveals the activity of love...life...the mystery of communion of "encounter," of coming together, of being face to face in the Infinite everywhere both hidden and unveiled in the manifestation: the ONE who gives is no different from the ONE who receives; the ONE who approaches is also approached; the ONE who loves is also loved.

Love, an active relationship, empowers our acts of compassion. The root of the word *compassion* is not the Latin *pietas* or "pity," but rather *cum patior,* which means "to share solidarity with," "to be in oneness with," "to undergo with." It has to arise from the awareness of the mutuality of all creatures, and according to some eminent biologists, the mutuality of every living form. Also, Dr. Ernest McCullough, a Canadian philosopher, points out that the way of compassion is found in shared suffering and also shared joy. The word *compassion* has lost some of its depth and vitality these days, and is most often relegated to the area of feeling. Compassion is deeper and more profound.

At the time I first wrote this (February 1986), Filipinos had just participated in a national turn-about, their Peoples' Power Revolution. It was an unplanned, un-orchestrated display of compassion and nonviolence. A display of love of country both by the People Power demonstrators and also by the military, who had a change of heart and defected.

In acting compassionately, both sides had to learn to use actions and terms that do not dichotomize. They heeded Martin Luther King's admonishing, "We avoid taking on the psychology of victors." And the incoming new president, Cory Aquino, did nothing to dehumanize the "other." She invited Marcos to make amends. A great insight in the adventure for me was that, as in The Sound of One Hand, in conflict there is no "other" at the deepest level. And that is the basis for all nonviolence.

But being nonviolent is not simply an intellectual decision. We must live so that we have access to that inner point, the still point, where communion is realized, and all walls are down. We also have to face the fact that the gift of relating to others at the level of integration is more gift than goal. It is not attained by an act of the will or by whim or by election.

For centuries, philosophers thought becoming non-violent impossible and improbable. Dr. McCullough says that philosophers from Cicero in ancient Rome to Husserl in the last century had difficulties with understanding the act of relating to others as an experience of integration with the consciousness of the "other." He says it was Husserl's disciple, Edith Stein, who, breaking through her own depression, experienced insights that found access to the deeper consciousness. Wittgenstein had a similar insight with the recognition that languages by their essence are public, hence experience transcends individual feelings. In Zen practice we come to discover that compassion and empathy are not feelings, they are activities. Edith Stein was eventually to define *empathy* as the experience of a foreign consciousness, an experience of quite a different order than the usually accepted feeling of compassion. It is of a more intimate dimension, more profound, and, in fact, an intimacy that is unitive.

It is an experience that should be very important for us Zen meditators, and for any teacher writing a teisho on The Sound of One Hand.

Indeed, to all the world, philosophically speaking, the One Hand reaches out in an act of awareness. Zen articulation of that activity would be reaching out and touching NOTHING, which is FULLNESS itself, and which brings us to a deeper and fuller understanding of what an act of awareness is.

There is hardly another word used as consistently in various Zen writings as the word *awareness*. It seems to be most often seen merely as the antithesis of daydreaming or lack of concentration. In reality, it is consciousness itself, not to be ignored, and recognized as an integration with the other world and other people.

I was recently asked just what "living in the present moment" really means. According to the specifics above, to live in the present moment means becoming aware of the quality of the relationship between yourself and the "other," and allowing that relationship to dissolve into union, communion. It also pre-supposes "Be-ing" where you are and "Do-ing" what you're doing. In less specific terms, any time you stray from your center and allow the ego to take over, you are not "living in the present moment." Our spirituality is working to break through obstacles, and gradually take on a receptive consciousness that allows the Presence within to operate. This power is intuitive and gratuitously endowed.

The Sound of One Hand is thusly working at all times. If it isn't, then we are superimposing our will and winning out. Nonviolence tells us that we never refer to ourselves as winners. It is not a temptation to do so when we "give in" to our Infinite guest, and let Be-ing *BE*. The one hand sounds beautifully in all such acts.

Perhaps in the past some of us have been too caught up in methods and goals. We need "organizing," which is people. In a letter to a young activist, Thomas Merton warned that in our work we can get caught up with expectations and results. In fact, to be a trained activist is to have your conscience raised through analysis and to be fired by ideals and with causes. But we easily get fed up with words and become emotionally drained. Empowerment comes from the center within, but the enacting techniques are frequently of great help.

We are not meant to pour ourselves out in the service of a dream. We are to live. To "live" in our work, says Thomas Merton, means that there is a lot that has to be gotten through, but we do gradually narrow it down more and more to specifics. Then it gets much more real. In the end, it is the reality of personal relationship that touches and saves everything.

The big results of our lives are not in your hands or mine but they suddenly happen and we can share in them. We cannot strive to build identities for ourselves in our work or our witness or both. Let us free ourselves from the domination of causes.

All that we do will come from the fact that we allowed ourselves to be used by a creative power. The real hope then is not something we think we can do, but in the power that is working through us.

At one point I was standing with demonstrators on Edsa Boulevard, next to a militant activitist, who got so angry at the people giving flowers and food to the soldiers. "How can they so quickly forget the military brutalities!" she cried. I replied, "They're not forgetting—they're forgiving!" The same power was working appropriately on *both* sides.

The Sound of One Hand will open the whole universe for us. It presupposes, though, freedom. Sitting should reduce our ego so that we are free to relate, but if the other ego is unfree and distended, there will be little interaction. Real empathy comes when both sides are free. That's why sometimes I suggest you "see" plants and animals during outdoor kinhin. They have no ego.

That's also why I suggest you taste deeply the interaction between you and those sitting with you in sesshin. All egos are down. You are meeting at a new level of universal intimacy. You can be called forth at that level, you can hear The Sound of One Hand—very easily. Let us be full of reply.

Part Two

The Miscellaneous Koans

Introduction

The immediate post-kensho period is usually rather trying for the Zen practitioner. The light of satori can be painful to the newly-opened third eye, and delving into the unfamiliar world of the koans can be rather vexing.

Koans by their nature are meant to be unsettling. One of their functions is to shake us from our established patterns of thought. Although there are several types of koans, it's fair to say about any of them that if it's reasonable, it's not a koan. And a koan is viewed from the Essential Nature point of view. As long as you go outside yourself, you'll not come to the appropriate presentation.

In the *Shitsunai Shirabe,* the dokusan-room study of koans, the first book used after completion of the Three Jewels is a small book of Miscellaneous Koans. These koans were assembled for use in the Haku'unkai, Yasutani Roshi's group of followers. My teacher, Yamada Roshi, also passed them on to his successors as an integral part of koan study.

Remembering my own painful beginnings, I decided to give these teisho to help the neophyte over the introduction to the various types of koans found in traditional Zen literature. These teisho were composed quickly over a period of a few months in 1981–1982. In 1985 and 2001, I went over them again. Now, in 2007, they are being made available to a wider readership.

Stop the sound
of the distant temple bell.

1

In our orientation talks, we defined a koan as *the presentation of a truth common to all, expressed in a riddle or conundrum form, which the intellect cannot accept.* In this first koan from the *Book of Miscellaneous Koans,* the conundrum seems to predominate. How ridiculous to think of stopping a bell that is ringing in a distant temple!

So, let's be a bit more specific. Let's say the distant temple is Enryakuji on Mount Hiei overlooking Kyoto in Japan. The main bell there is set off by itself on a small arm of the lovely Hieian hillside. The structure upholding and surrounding it is almost another building. There is a broad staircase of about fifty steps leading up to it. How can you stop that bell from ringing when it is so far away?

Consider the following koan, in which a famous Chinese Zen master is asking the "seeker" before him the leading question found in Zen mondo:

Master:	Where have you come from?
Disciple:	I've come from India.
Master:	When did you leave there?
Disciple:	I left this morning.
Master:	What took you so long?

Now remember, that mondo took place over a thousand years ago. No chance of jet transportation between India and China in half a day. The reply is in the spirit of Theravada Buddhism, where the piling up of *joriki,* the power of the concentrated mind, is encouraged.

Levitation and self-propelled air journeys, as a result of concentration, are altogether possible, you know.

One of the zendo members once told me that she had received a notice from the Transcendental Meditation Headquarters, offering a course—to instruct the TM teachers how to levitate. What is levitation for? Who are you helping flying around in the air? Considering this, we come to a touch of the pragmatic in our stream of Zen, the way of Mahayana Buddhism, in which our practice has nothing to do with air journeys, whether by levitation or jet-propelled planes. But still, the distance problem has to be solved, obviously.

Now let's consider the bell.

How familiar are you with bells? In the rural Philippines, a bell is often a piece of suspended metal, hit with a stone. Since this is not very resonant, the striking is done rather persistently and the result is *BANG–BANG–BANG–BANG–BANG–BANG–BANG!* It is almost impossible to remain lying in bed as those sounds flood the town or barrio in the early Sunday hours. Or the high *ding-a-ling-a-ling* we can sometimes hear outside our window in summer—probably the ice cream truck.

In Europe and North America we have a long tradition of bells ringing very round sounds. We have small bells ringing *DING, DING, DING.* And we have large bells ringing *DONG, DONG, DONG.* And we have a combination of small bells and larger bells ringing together *DING–DONG–DING–DONG–DING–DONG.*

We have a whole range of sounds in the carillons, with many bells that can ring out a complete melody. One of the musts of New York City is to hear the bells of Riverside Church, between Columbia and the old Juilliard School of Music. Every Sunday morning, they chime out a complete concert for about an hour—a joyful peak of resonances.

I daresay that the most famous bells in the whole world are the set in the tower of Big Ben in London, England. They have been chiming out the hours and the quarter hours for centuries to the whole world, as all "time" is regulated from the worthy and nearby Greenwich Mean....*DING–DING–DING–DONG; DING–DING–DING–DING–DING–DING–DONG; DING–DING–DING–DING–DONG! DONG! DONG!* Three o'clock in Greenwich, some o'clock everywhere.

Now, as I said before, our koan refers to a bell in a Japanese temple. If you have been to Japan you will know that a temple bell is shaped something like a pear. Its height is about that of an ordinary person. It is suspended on a framework that must necessarily be of rather generous proportions. A wooden pole, about four inches in diameter, is suspended horizontally, at a point slightly lower than the middle of the bell. The Buddhist priest (or bell ringer) pulls the rope holding the pole, and a deep dark round sound comes forth—*BONG*. It's a long sound, very resonant—*BONG*. The reverberations go on and on and are carried into infinity. A temple bell is very sacred; it is never rung quickly. The sound is usually not repeated until the vibrations of the first are completed and gone to their rest. *BONG*. It is an introverted sound and will descend to the very depths of your being. *BONG*.

Now, are you comfortable with that bell? First you have to ring it. And then you've got to stop it. Ridiculous, isn't it? And what truth could it possibly be pointing at?

Using Yamada Roshi's terminology, we have to look at the bell in both its aspects—its phenomenal nature and its Essential Nature. The phenomenal side we can see with our two eyes. We can see the height, guess the weight, hear the sound, feel the metal. But the other aspect, the Essential Nature, can only be "seen" with our third eye, which has opened a little bit in a kensho realization. This experience is the only key that will help you present this koan in the dokusan room.

The problem of course is that as long as the bell is ringing in Japan, you can't stop it—distance seems to be quite a deterrent! Our mind can bridge that distance very easily. But we know our mind cannot solve a koan.

Now, the point of this koan is "to *stop* the bell." This refers directly to the Gateless Gate—the Essential World. In order to understand it better, let's look at the phenomenal world for a moment. Mumon says, "Things that come in through the gate are not family treasures. What is gained by causation is continuously going on, forming and disintegrating." Things that come in through the gate can mean knowledge gained through the intellect. In our daily world, we can stop things by pressing a button. *FLICK!*—and you can turn on the radio. *PUSH!*—and a nuclear holocaust could start the same way. We *know* if we flick in reverse, or "not-push," we forestall war. We can stop and start in the phenomenal world.

Now, the family treasure Mumon is talking about is, of course, our Essential Nature. Here we are talking about another world, which is totally empty. When we look at the world from the Essential Point of "stopped," there is nothing to be seen at all—nothing to be started or stopped, nothing to be "put out."

Most people are at home in the phenomenal world. But very few people even know that the Essential World exists. Zen treats things from the Essential point of view; and therefore koans should be approached this way.

Let us read Yamada Roshi's teaching on the Essential Nature from Case 4 of the *Gateless Gate:*

> What is this Essential Nature? Who has it? What is it like?
>
> All existence has its Essential Nature—every person, every thing, the whole universe. There is no difference between people's Essential Nature and the Essential Nature of things and the universe. It is all the same. When you attain True Self-realization, you will acknowledge that this is true. There is no dualistic opposition in the Essential Nature, such as subject and object, good and bad, Buddha and ordinary person, enlightenment and delusion.
>
> The Essential Nature has no form, no color, no weight, no length, no place, no concepts, no taint or blemish attached to it. It is perfectly pure.
>
> The Essential Nature cannot be destroyed, even by karmic fire. If the whole universe were to be completely destroyed, the Essential Nature would continue to exist because it is empty. It is non-substantial. It cannot be seen with the eyes, heard with the ears, or touched with the hands. No one can identify the spot where it is.
>
> We cannot locate our Essential Nature because it is zero, yet it has infinite capabilities. It can see with eyes, walk with legs, think with a brain, and digest food with a stomach. It weeps when it is sad, and laughs when it is happy. Though it is zero, no one can deny its existence. It is one with phenomena. The Essential Nature and phenomena are one from the very beginning. That is why the *Hannya Shingyo*, the Heart Sutra, can say, "Form is nothing but emptiness; emptiness is nothing but form."
>
> Yet our Essential Nature is not a thought or a philosophical concept. It cannot be grasped by our physical senses, but it is our existing reality. It can be comprehended only in direct

experience. This experience is kensho or satori, the enlightenment of Zen.

Now if our physical senses cannot grasp the Essential Nature, how are we going to stop from acting? We cannot. There is no stopping or starting in the Essential World. Not that it is inert but it is empty. We can describe *IT* as "unifying dynamism," but there is no coming or going.

This is stated in Hakuin Zenji's *Wasan*: "going and coming, [we are] never astray." Also we have the words of T.S. Eliot from his poem "Burnt Norton":

> *...at the still point, there the dance is,*
> *But neither arrest nor movement. And do not call it fixity,*
> *Where past and future are gathered. Neither movement*
> *   from nor towards,*
> *Neither ascent nor decline. Except for the point, the still point,*
> *There would be no dance, and there is only the dance.*

The "stopping" of the bell is a kind of hook in the koan. Don't bite on it and get caught. Our experience of life shows us usually only the phenomenal world, which separates us from bells. In our Zen practice, we must become prophets—those who see and proclaim things as they are. But you will not see as a prophet until you cut down the separations. Until you close the gap between you and Mu, you will never discover what Mu is. You will never *know* God, human beings, or creation until your knowing becomes experience.

This is delightfully illustrated in the following Buddhist story of the little salt doll, who was confronted with two worlds.

THE STORY OF THE LITTLE SALT DOLL

Once upon a time, there was a little doll made of salt who had made a long pilgrimage on dry land. One day she came to the sea, which was something she had never seen before. Here she found herself confronting a phenomenon she felt she could not possibly know or understand. There she was, a little solid doll of salt, standing on firm ground, watching another sort of ground that was not firm at all, but was moving and insecure and noisy and strange and unknown. She felt she could never get to know or understand it.

Nevertheless, the little doll walked right up to the edge of the sea and asked, "What are you?"

The sea replied, "I am me."

The doll said, "I've never seen anything like you before. I don't know you at all. I'd like to, though. Please help me and tell me how I can come to know you."

The sea answered, "Touch me."

The little doll shyly put forth her foot and touched the water. Oh, how different! She felt a unique thing happening, and knew she was somewhat lighter, something she had never experienced before. But it did give her the feeling that the sea could be knowable. She withdrew her leg, and as it came out of the water, she could see that her toes had disappeared.

"What have you done to me?" she cried.

The sea replied kindly, "You have given something in order to understand."

At first the doll was disconcerted, and wasn't sure just how profitable this exchange really was. But she *did* feel better, and went into the sea again, a little further, so that she would understand more deeply. Once again the sea took away more of her salt. Strangely enough, this gave her a liberated feeling, so she went farther and farther into the sea. At each succeeding moment she seemed to understand more deeply, although all the while she was losing more of her salt. Her determination kept her going, and so did that ultimate question, "But what *is* the sea?"

Finally, a big wave engulfed her, and as it dissolved the rest of her salt, the little doll cried out in great happiness, "Now I know what the sea is...*It is I!*"

Put out the fire
a thousand miles away.

2

This is a koan at its best, and one that a good Zen teacher will request in the dokusan room.

Perhaps we have all had some experience in putting out a fire. If we really do that, we are object to it, or it is object to us. That is, it is only in the phenomenal world.

As is stated time and again in teisho, koans usually deal with the Essential World. The Essential World is often designated as the unseen world of One-ness. But, you know, that is not satisfactory. First, because it is not factual to the experience; second, "one" is the beginning of a sequence of numbers that specify the phenomenal world—that of form and color. Third, One-ness is a kind of existence, an entity. There is no thing in the Essential World. Or as we so often say, perhaps more accurately, it is the world of no-thing–ness. For example, we can consider a line in the Bible that seems to present two: Whoever rejects me rejects the one who sent me (Luke 10:16). That "one" is an entity and is presented as such and stands against the "me." Such a statement can be processed by the intellect. It is not no-thing. But after my many years in Zen, I can see and be aware of the "One-ness" that is pointing at "not-two." The mystics of old considered the word *advaita* (Sanskrit for "not two") as being true to the experience.

I stress this here because many people tell me they have had an experience of "being one with God." I'm sure they are very sincere and have had some kind of an intimate personal revelation. I said in *Light Sitting in Light* that if I am speaking to a group of thirty-five people and mention "God" then thirty-five gods appear on the screen of their consciousnesses. The Absolute we touch in the kensho experience seems to be realized on its own terms. It's an experience of something totally new. I have never met anyone with a confirmed breakthrough who did not express surprise. As I often say, when someone touches a live wire all the things written and spoken about electricity are of little help in understanding. An experience of union is part and parcel of kensho; but we have so many possible venues of union through the *kokoro* (soul) that Zen teachers are wary of that lone articulation—but I am running away from the koan.

"Put out the fire a thousand miles away." This koan comprises three things: (1) a verb—"put out" or "extinguish"; (2) a fire burning brightly; (3) a distance—one thousand miles away. From what I said previously, you will perhaps be able to make some sense of the verb. We have to extinguish or put out. Already that seems to me to be pointing to the Essential World because it is demanding extinction, getting rid of things.

I sometimes recommend the book *No Boundaries* by Ken Wilbur. In this book, he says something that I think we can all truthfully admit—that we seem to operate within boundaries. Some people are very head-bound. Some are heart-bound. We are inclined to be very skin-bound too. It is commonplace for us to consider ourselves to be encompassed by our actual physical boundary.

But Zen teaches us that we have another dimension in which we are not bound at all. That is another characteristic of kensho—in that experience, we come to realize that our head-boundary and skin-boundary have disappeared. This is necessary if we are to be graced by the breakthrough to "not-two." I have a set of graphics showing a drop of water entering the ocean. Eventually it loses its boundaries. The fine line that makes it a raindrop disappears or is extinguished or put out. And there is the Zen-like quotation: "The joy of the raindrop is to enter the ocean." I smiled at the liturgical reading from Job (19:21–27): "and after my skin has been destroyed, then in my flesh I shall see God." The destroying of the boundaries in kensho was described by Dogen Zenji as "the falling away of body and mind."

The graphics I referred to contain a couple of very arresting pictures of raindrops entering the ocean, and show the pull of the ocean as it seems to go up to meet the descending, disintegrating raindrop. There is a pull at work.

In a letter I received from the wife of one of the prisoners in contact with the Prison Phoenix Trust (PPT)* she told me she had started to

---

*Prison Phoenix Trust encourages prisoners in the UK to use their cell as a place of spiritual practice, using meditation and yoga. Sister Elaine was Director from 1992–1999.

meditate and participate in the same discipline as her husband. This is what she wrote: "I meditate when I know my husband is doing so, and since we are meditating together, I do not feel separated from him in any way."

If a koan is to deal with the Essential World, then you have to extinguish or put out any "thing" that might exist in the world. You know, our mind can put things in and out of anywhere. I recall saying in teisho during a sesshin that one Zen master used to say that we are all made from the same cookie dough—and in dokusan one of the sitters said her mind was indeed a cookie-cutter! If we have developed our mind it becomes very clever. But even if we haven't, it is still very active and discriminatory.

Next we deal with the fire that is mentioned in the koan. Fire gives us many blessings: light and heat, for instance. And Proverbs (40:3–5) asks us, "Where is the way to the dwelling of light?" The conundrum is very prominent. We could very well approach the koan from that point of view.

I would like to invite you to enter that light, to be that heat. My friend and mentor, Ruben Habito, used to say, "not to think but to *be* is the secret of koans." When it comes to heat, I recall my thousands of experiences in the Japanese bath, the *ofuro*. There is a koan in the Hekiganroku (The Blue Cliff Record) that says that sixteen bodhisattvas each had a breakthrough when they entered the ofura on one occasion. Of course, on the one hand, they were ready. But on the other, they were also "open"...open to the *IT* of this ofuro. But suffice it to say here that I think most of the time when "mindfulness" is used in Zen texts "openness" to and from the Source is meant. And the Zen practice could also be more tactile. It is said the catalyst to a breakthrough usually comes through one of the senses. So keep them open!

My mother was a wood-artist. Our living room held an array of antique chairs and tables, and my sisters and I discovered, to our dismay, that they all required a different kind of wood polish! Nevertheless, I distinctly recall Mother telling us one day, "If you like a piece of wood and want to touch it, do so. Feel it well. And receive what it has to give you!"

My suggestion to you when engaging this koan is to enter "heat" or "fire" whenever you meet it. Feel it. Taste it. Be aware of it. Linger for a moment. This is true for all the senses. Stop to smell the flowers, as the saying goes.

There is a Zen teaching that says when you are in pain, *be the pain!* In fact, the old texts say, kill yourself with the pain. By that they mean that you kill the process we human beings usually go through when we are in pain. It seems normal for us to fight the pain. Stop fighting, your practice is saying. Just *be the pain*. Heat and fire are no different.

The last part of the koan has to do with distance, separation: one thousand miles away. That is in the phenomenal world. You have to bring it into the Essential, if you are in koan study. There (or should I say, "Here") is no problem. You have to overcome that distance.

Distance is no separation. There is no wall of separation like a prison wall. One of my prisoner disciples wrote:

> We are locked in our individual cells daily from 8 p.m. until 8 a.m. I sit every night and find these evenings very conducive to deep sitting, even though it is almost impossible to do kinhin (walking meditation) since the length of the cell is only three steps and there is no width! But one night I sat for a couple of hours, and then as I was doing one such kinhin, all the tensions and inner struggles dissolved into nothing, and a new boundless Union only existed! At that particular moment, instantaneous yet infinite, I was awakened to the Essential World! Right now the prison walls are down, and I am roaming and romping about! At the crack of dawn, the surroundings are resplendent, and the fields are verdant. In a short while we will wake up to a new spring when everything will be new!

Our new-seeing eyes will provide us with the joy of seeing the familiar for the first time.

*Stop the boat sailing by
out on the open sea.*

3

Here we have another fine koan. Stop the boat sailing by. You will notice the similarity with the first and second koans: stop the bell ringing in Japan, and put out the fire a thousand miles away. In all three instances, we are extinguishing something. I hope you are familiar enough with Zen texts to immediately recognize that that is a desired event. To extinguish, to wipe out, eliminate, eradicate, erase—in other words, "to empty."

The way to work on a koan is not to bring it into the light and examine it. The intellect cannot solve a koan. The memory cannot solve a koan. Our emotions cannot solve a koan. Our imagination cannot solve a koan. Our will cannot solve a koan.

None of these instruments of light (as I call them) can bring us to the enlightenment we seek in Zen sitting. So how do we work on a koan? We do so by entering the silence and the darkness all alone and allowing the koan to find us. That is why the first three koans in this little book speak of *extinguishing*. I want to speak of that today.

Zen speaks of the Essential World always as the dark. In the dark we cannot see anything. In a way, we are blind—and Zen would say a good kind of blindness. And since this Essential World is the world of no-thing, if we want to enter that world and experience *IT*, then we have to extinguish all things *interiorly*. (The catalyst comes from without.) That, as you well know by now, is extinguishing all thoughts and desires and memories and plans, and so on, and just *be-ing* in the dark silence.

Darkness is often presented as undesirable in our culture. It is seen as the place and stuff of fear and the unknown. But for people who either *see* or are endeavoring to *see*, darkness is friendly.

43

Listen to what Rilke has to say in his *Book of Hours:*

You darkness, of whom I am born—

I love you more than the flame
that limits the world
to the circle it illumines...

In Zen, emptying is automatically accomplished little by little when we sit in inner silence. And you often hear that sitting dissolves inner blocks. I once had a disciple who had a problem with anger, a deep explosive anger. He was a father of two sons, and told me early in our relationship that he was afraid of what he might do to one of them in a fit of anger. I had no other help for him except that he sit and let the anger dissolve. He followed that advice and the desired change occurred.

Sitting does remove some of our deep-seated problems. It also works as a kind of cleansing agent that removes the stickiness. There is something strong and clean about sitting. When we sit well and continuously, there is a cleansing that purifies and purges. I choose those words because they suggest the result of that cleansing—namely, nonattachment.

The instruments of light, which I spoke of above, attract objects. Intellect—we think of something. Memory—we recall something. Emotions—we go out in love. Will—we decide to carry something through. Imagination—we create something. These are their functions. They are not bad, but they make us liable (so Shakyamuni says) to start desiring the objects. Shakyamuni taught that all suffering comes from desiring. And desiring brings a kind of stickiness into our souls. Separating ourselves from those objects, as we do in meditation, is time spent in nonattachment; it becomes part of our practice.

My assistant and I gave a workshop once to twenty-four lifers at Wormwood Scrubs Prison in London, England. It ended with a particularly good meditation, from which the men did not seem to want to be disturbed. So I quoted Yamada Roshi: "We are all born to be mystics." There was not a snicker of disbelief among them.

I am not a student of comparative religions and cannot speak for the writings of all mystics. But I can speak for Buddhism and Christianity, and on the common ground on which their mysticism is taught and understood. The mystics of both religions state frequently and unequivocally that nonattachment is the measuring rod for the depth of our practice. And I remember so well Yamada Roshi's words when I first went to him—"You are a violinist, an artist. Do not be attached to beauty. You must go beyond that."

I will say something about Christianity. The mysticism experienced and practiced by the Rhineland mystics seems to be the closest to their Asian counterparts. I have been feasting on the writings of Eckhart and Tauler and Rysbroeck. Here is what Eckhart says of non-Christian mystics:

> I have read many writings of heathen philosophers and sages of the old covenant and the new, and have sought earnestly and with all diligence which is the best and highest virtue whereby a man may knit himself most narrowly to God, and wherein he is most like to his exemplar, as he was in God, wherein there was no difference between himself and God before God created creatures. Having pondered these scriptures to the best of my ability, I find it none other than absolute detachment [nonattachment]...he who would be serene and pure needs just one thing—detachment.

Nonattachment is freedom. Not to be stuck. Recently, I tried to mend the top of a terra cotta green tea pot with superglue. I was stuck for two hours—both hands and two pieces of pot! Unfree!

Nonattachment is the epitome, for it cleanses the soul, clarifies the mind, kindles the heart, and wakes the spirit. It quickens desire for the Ultimate and enhances virtue, giving in to the intuition of God, in experience.

Eckhart says he extols detachment above any love. He says the old masters laud humility above most other virtues, but he ranks detachment before any meekness. Perfect nonattachment is without regard, without either lowliness or loftiness. It has no mind to be below or yet to be above. It is minded to be master of itself.

Now let's return to the koan, to the boat on the open sea. Once again there is the twin problem of object and distance, both of which have to be extinguished. Remember, it's the boat in your head, the picture of the boat that is problematic—if you could bring a canoe into the dokusan room, there might not be such a problem at all!

As far as the sea is concerned, for me it is the place of rendezvous par excellence. I had occasion recently to write:

It finally happened: that millennial search for root connections. I was barefoot in the sand dunes on Canada's east coast; barefoot because my Zen studies teach that we can make direct connections through the soles of the feet, and on Canada's coast because of my ancient affinity with the sea. That day, I was being, or as I experienced it then, BE-ING, one with the cooling grains inserting themselves between my toes. One with the smell of the sea. One with the waves as they teased both ear and eye to intimacy.

And then suddenly it happened. The connection was made. It was as though my hand had been taken and given a gentle squeeze. I had to smile, understanding why I perceived it all in capital letters, the sacred, the personal, beloved and known. In a flash, I remembered a moment over twenty-five years before in Japan, when a Japanese Zen master had confirmed my opening meditative experience, into a world I had never experienced before, a world of no things and no boundaries, but a world at one with my happy pounding heart.

I was invited to write about that realization and a few days later, with pen in hand and almost without thinking, the first words came out…"I was born by the sea." Even at the time, I immediately considered that unpremeditated statement. Why did I write it? I knew it came from a truth, but was nevertheless surprised at its immediacy and certainty. And it was not only referring to location, but to experience. And what I experienced was referred to by the roshi as a "fact," partly because he was sometimes impatient with my frequent use of the word mystery. We Christians seem to love that designation and all the baggage it carries. Zen speaks of fact, and a fact is a fact with nothing sticking to it. So those six words were a fact for me. I was born by the sea.

I suppose it is to be expected that a Pisces who always likes the feel of moving through water would sooner or later in Zen come upon the fact of the water. I found it to be not only a sensuous experience, but also the location of the transcendent.

Water is eminently a place of rendezvous! I have since discovered that there are many adherents (even some not born under Pisces!) who belong to the secret community of sea-intimates. And it is almost commonplace that these protagonists find their life-discipline in meditation. All of them are aware of the connection. It is a kind of home acceptance with the surge of deep waters. Canada's environment-friendly scientist David Suzuki has said that life is animated water. That movement of the sea is, in more ways than one, identical to the deep inner longing and restlessness in the depths of our soul. But it wasn't until three-quarters of a century later that I realized I was born with that longing.

Of course, our place of transcendence is always just where we are at the moment, even the boat of this koan. Can you stop it as it passes by?

Save a ghost.

4

On the subject of ghosts, this Canadian always feels pretty much poverty-stricken. When I lived in Leyte Island in the Philippines, I found that ghosts abounded. Not too far from our convent, there was a large acacia tree that harbored a *wakwak* (as the local ghosts were called); and to pass near that tree after dark was risky. To go near it after you'd had a drink of chocolate was lethal.

I almost had an encounter with a ghost shortly after I went to Leyte to live in 1977. We were just getting into our barrio project there, and many group meetings were necessary. One morning I went to attend the one scheduled, and I couldn't find anyone in the hall. I went to the home of Tilde, the project leader, and found it completely shuttered. I called out, and one shutter opened a fraction. Tilde informed me that the night before, a young lad near Laida's house had committed suicide, and, naturally, no one would be about for eleven days. I couldn't believe my ears, and with accustomed Canadian stamina, I debated the issue and its consequences for several minutes. I asked Tilde to take me to the distressed home, which she did, more than a little unwillingly. No one was there. We went back to Laida's house, and she admonished Tilde to go back to her own house immediately.

Then Laida started to instruct me about ghosts. "He was here a few minutes ago," she said. "There was a knock at the door and I just stared at it. And then the door opened, and I could hear his feet as he came in. He walked right in front of me, went over to that chair over there, and I could see the cushion go down as he settled into it." She lowered her voice. "I just stood there and didn't say a word. Then he got up and went over to the table, and since there was no food there, he went to the door again, opened it, went out, and I could hear his footsteps as he went down the path."

Now I ask you, What is an unbelieving Canadian going to do when confronted by such evidence? I tell you what I did do—I had a much better grasp of this koan.

What is a ghost to you? Webster's says that a ghost is "a disembodied soul of a dead person, believed to be an inhabitant of the unseen world, or to appear to the living in bodily likeness." Let's try the Oxford dictionary: "the soul of a dead person in Hades; dead person appearing to the living; apparition, spectre, emaciated person, shadowy outline or semblance." It sees the word *ghostly* as having to do with sacred or ecclesiastical matters.

I am spending time on the meaning of the word, just in case, like me, you are ignorant about ghosts, but are still expected to present this koan in the dokusan room. I well recall going into the dokusan room and telling Yamada Roshi that I didn't know very much about ghosts. He said, "Japanese ghosts hold resentments, have grievances; they torment people because they cannot go to heaven."

The next word I want to treat for a moment is *save*. Those who do a lot of reading of Buddhist texts quite often come across this word. This enters a whole area of possible contention, and I prefer to use the verb *to free* instead. And the koan becomes less of a hurdle for us Westerners if we look at it in the sense that "to save" or "to free" means to help the ghost.

We help a ghost the same way we help others, whether human beings or animals or things, by realizing our oneness with them. Now you may be mentally involved with all kinds of peripheral impediments in being involved with a ghost. But remember, we all suffer the fundamental delusion of separation. We all probably admit to this. But are we aware of another fundamental delusion that keeps us isolated, separate from others? That fundamental delusion is ego. We can't see our oneness with the so-called "other" if we are full of ego. There is no room, so to speak. That is why we stress "emptying" in Zen. Emptying is a process we have to work at.

I often wonder if we are aware of the number of times we strengthen our ego. Every time we assert our individuality, we strengthen the ego. Every time we put ourselves in opposition, we strengthen the ego. Every time we ask to do something different from the established order in the zendo, we strengthen the ego. Many moments of self-preoccupation are ego-centered.

Once, I was at a gathering at which several zendo members were present. I heard a guest ask one of them, "What is your goal in Zen?" The answer was, "to find my True Self." This did not sit well with the listener, who came to me immediately protesting such an ego-centered goal. Unfortunately, she was so busy describing her own altruistic goal, I never had the opportunity to explain what the zendo member probably meant. But the gist of the question was not without basis. On face value, "to find my True Self" does have the ego showing a bit. Let's look at that for a moment.

When I went to study in Kamakura, I was not given a load of concepts or even philosophy. All that was asked was that I be a human being, choose Zen as my way, and practice under a qualified teacher. Zen teaching is not heavy or complex. As I look back now, I see that three *kanji* (Japanese ideograms) put it all together for me. I want to speak of one of those kanji now, *kokoro* in Japanese. There is no adequate English equivalent word. Most dictionaries, however, translate it as "mind," which covers only a small portion of the breadth of its reality.

Kokoro comes from the Sanskrit *hridaya,* which contains a wealth of meaning and feeling. It points to the very core of our being and to what is best, dearest, and most sacred there. It is the deep "you" and harbors at the same time a feeling of the Japanese *natsukashii,* or "homesickness."

When I was in England, I was given a poem by the seventeenth-century poet George Herbert, entitled "The Pulley." A pulley, as you know, is a wheel for lifting weights or changing directions. In his poem, Herbert sees the pulley as an appropriate metaphor for the gift or blessing by which we can handle the heavy times that life sometimes brings us. Also, as in the case of prisoners with whom I used to work, a pulley has the faculty of helping us change directions when we find ourselves traveling opposite to our best interests. Herbert's poem reads in part:

> *When God first made man*
> *Having a glass of blessings standing by,*
> *Let us, said he, pour on man*
> *All the world's riches that we can.*

So, strength first made a way
Then beauty flowed
Then wisdom, honour, pleasure.

And then the poem goes on to say that God purposely withheld one blessing, and that was the gift of satisfaction or complete rest, with the words:

let him keep the rest,
but keep them with repining restlessness.

Not only ghosts are restless, but we living human beings are as well. The Japanese people, Asian spirituality, and my Celtic ancestors all seem to take this "repining restlessness" for granted. Certainly the Japanese word *natsukashii* catches the feeling. The Orient seems to be telling us that in our ordinary everyday mind and heart, we have to deal with this longing. Another way of looking at the goal of Zen meditation is that it brings us to an experience of knowing what we are longing for! I have often wondered whether or not the moaning ghost of this koan knew what she or he was longing for!

Perhaps we Zen sitters can say that all our answers are within. If we are truly empty of ego, then there is a chance that the appropriate measure will be given. Even with a full satori experience, there is the all-surpassing hole that we can fall into, the hole of not recognizing the pull to help the needy. Therein lies the meaning of *bodhisattva,* someone who goes around doing appropriate good for the needy. Our capacity, our place of practice, our *dojo,* is right here and now, to help us develop a capacity for emptiness and living in harmony with our original innermost longings.

A dojo is something like a gymnasium. It is a place for stretching a little bit. A place tending toward the spartan, marked by self-discipline and avoidance of luxury and comfort. We say in the orientation talks that Zen is not asceticism. Shakyamuni found that asceticism didn't work. But Zen is not self-indulgence either. In his orientation talks, Aitken Roshi says, "The practice involves rigor, and is not possible in a casual lifestyle."

Zen is the middle way, in which we must keep pushing ourselves bit by bit. This will, of course, involve pain. Yamada Roshi used to say that pain in the legs is a taste of Zen. Sometimes he would add with a smile as he looked around the zendo, "I wonder if you know what I mean!" Anyone who has participated in a sesshin, a week-long retreat, knows.

Shakyamuni's whole life was spent in the name of suffering. He taught that fighting suffering or trying to avoid it leads to worse suffering. It hurts to face life sometimes, so people drink alcohol excessively and cause greater hurts. It hurts to share the wealth, so people create poverty to protect their comfortable greed.

Aitken Roshi used to give good advice. "Sit at the forward edge of your physical endurance," he would say. "Some people baby themselves. Where there is physical resistance, there is usually spiritual resistance." It might be helpful here to mention that physical conditions in a zendo are decided by the roshi or the *jikijitsu*. By that I mean anything to do with heat or light or opening windows, and so on. There is always a divergence of opinion on these matters, so they are left to the discretion of those responsible in an individual dojo. Giving over the decision will help keep the decision-making apparatus still, the ego down, and your focus on the inner Presence.

At the end of the day, each of us has to decide our own middle way. And if we sit at the forward edge of our endurance, then at that point we will not be static. Here in this room at this moment, we have our own dojo. For the rest of the week we must make our own. It is everywhere you go. And our ghost is hunting for that dojo. Can you help it?

Move a mountain.

5

The other day I was reading a book, *Theravada and Zen,* and the author, Bhikku Ananda, was obviously a dedicated and sincere advocate of the former, Theravada, trying desperately to understand the latter, Zen. He says, superficially indeed:

> Zen may seem so different to the Theravadin that he may dogmatically assert that Zen is not Buddhism. One cannot blame a Theravadin for all that he sees and criticizes in Zen, for he is brought up in an entirely different atmosphere. There are some things in Zen so bizarre, as to scare and frighten the pious literary followers of early Buddhism and make them feel and declare that whatever Zen might be, it is not Buddhism. For instance, in the records of Zen, we may come across an earnest pupil monk who, wishing to know the truth, would seek the help of his Zen master and ask, "Who is Buddha?" The Zen master rather bluntly replies, "The cat climbs the post." Bewildered and confused at the master's reply, the pupil monk confesses his inability to grasp the meaning, to which the Zen master says again, "If you don't understand me, ask the post!"
>
> To the Theravadin it would naturally occur, as it may have to the Zen novice, "What does the cat's climbing the post, or the post itself, have to do with Buddhism"' The reply, which seems to have no bearing on the question, would scare the Theravadan Buddhist.

I am not a student of comparative religions, and therefore do not know how true this reaction would be for other great religions of the world, but I *do* know that it would not, or should not, be true for Christians. If a Christian asked a Zen master, "Who is God?" and the Zen master replied, "The cat climbs the post," the Christian might feel confused and be unable to respond, but should never be scared or frightened, or think this reply bizarre! He or she might even be heard to murmur, "Here we go again!" For a Christian who has any familiarity at all with the words of Scripture has been exposed to such verbal outrages since youth:

> "Taking a piece of bread in his hands, he said, 'This is my body.'"
> "If you had faith you could say to this mulberry tree, be rooted up and replanted in the sea, and it would obey you."
> "The Kingdom of God is within you."

Or the koan that all the evangelists, and Paul, used, "If you had faith the size of a mustard seed [and of course it has just been explained that the mustard seed is the smallest of all seeds] you could *move a mountain!*"

If Paul had been a Zen master, he would probably have phrased it this way, "If you want to increase your faith, move a mountain," just the way any other Zen master is sure to ask in the dokusan room. To move a mountain. A formidable task indeed!

What is a mountain? The other day I heard a little girl say that a mountain is a valley upside down. And she's essentially right. Mountains and valleys are not different when you look at them in a certain way. But then, neither are they the same. There are no mountains in the world that are essentially high, not even Mount Everest; and by the same token, they are not low either. And of course in the Philippines there is the delightful experience of being able to stand on the banks of the lake at Tagaytay and *look down* on Taal Mountain and exclaim, "It's high, isn't it?"

The trouble with mountains is that they are always "over there." We tend to step back from them to get the full view. And it's true, the further away you get from Mount Fuji, the more beautiful it is! Anyone who has climbed it will say that its beauty is nowhere to be seen as it is mounted, one weary step after the other. However, if you are swimming in one of the surrounding lakes and see its towering majesty, you not only "meet" its beauty, you are moved by it. Now that's the first hint.

A mountain can move us. It calls forth something in us: "How beautiful!" What is that "something"? Is it something that can be reversed into us moving the mountain, instead of it moving us?

Another problem with mountains is that we are always confronted with their size. They tend to be big and heavy. We can't get close enough to lift them. And even if we could, we wouldn't be able to bear their weight. But here again there is hope. In the Bible, the prophet Isaiah tells us that God knows the weight of all the earth, and has weighed all the mountains and hills. God might be a good source to go to in solving the koan. And that's a second hint.

In the dokusan room, people tend to become loquacious when they start trying to move a mountain. They will reminisce about a mountain in their childhood, about how they feel on a certain mountain they climbed in their teenage years. Some people resort to clever words and take the mountain apart rock by rock! And the desperate become quite eloquent, "I feel one with the mountain," or "I *am* one with the mountain," and ultimately, "I've moved it,"—all the while being unmoved and unmovable, as they sit there burdened with the mountain.

A kind teacher, trying to help, will ask the perennial Zen question, "Which is higher, Tibet's Mount Everest or the Philippine's Mount Mayon?" Only a rank beginner would say "Mount Everest." Everyone knows Zen is not a study in comparative adjectives or mountains, and the state of speechlessness that usually follows this question is a good state to be in. As long as your mind is boggled and your mouth speechless, there is a chance that your ears will open, because the mountain is not speechless. It has a word it utters ceaselessly! What is the word of the mountain? In the words of the Zen master quoted at the beginning: "Ask the mountain."

Father Oshida, O.P., a Zen man living in the mountain west of Tokyo, wrote in *The Mystery of the Word and Reality:*

> When a farmer takes care of rice-fields, he does not run to the library each year to research the events of rice cultivation. He listens to the rice because it will talk to him and tell him whether or not water and fertilizer are lacking, and whether or not it is too cold! The fact of the rice is the word!

In the same way, the fact of the mountain is the word. Can you say it? Can you hear it? It's the same word that the nun Jissai asked Gutei to utter (Mumonkan, Case 3); the same word that Nansen asked for, so that he would not kill the cat (Mumonkan, Case 14); or when he drew a circle on the ground and said to his friends, "If you can say a word, we will go on to see Chu Kokushi" (Hekiganroku, Case 69).

The way to hear the word is to get above the discriminating thoughts about the mountain. It does not concern itself whether the mountain is high or low, heavy or light, a Buddhist or a Christian mountain. Remember, the word of the mountain is a fact, a word-fact that absorbs the contradictions of high and low, heavy and light, Buddhist and Christian.

Despite the fact that mountains are unsettling things, they have a call of their own. Listen, if you have ears to hear. Close the distance. Solve its mystery! Learn its secret!

Sister Angelita Gutierrez was the second person to enter the Philippine zendo, back in August 1976. Speaking of her search, her attempt to conquer that mountain, she says:

> In real loneliness, I searched and searched until I wanted to weep. But the lingering presence [of the mountain] wooed me and the more I ran, the emptier I became. It took a long time before I discovered I must just keep still, and I would be found. He [it] was not the object of my search, I was.

There's no doubt about it. A mountain is a good place to find yourself, your True Self. In almost all religions we find a mountain as the place of revelation. For example, from the Psalms we learn that mountains came forth from the hand of God, who made them witnesses to his power. And the very charter of Christianity (which Aitken Roshi's group in Tacoma, Washington, calls "The Dharma of the Lord Jesus") has always been known as "The Sermon on the Mount." It was on the Mountain of Tabor that Christ revealed his Inner Self. And it was on a mountain that Christ chose his twelve apostles, who were to carry on his work and accomplish their missions. He went to a mountain when he wanted to pray alone. And it was on Mount Calvary that he spilled out for us everything he had. Christianity's most famous mountain climber, John of the Cross, called his mountain Mount Carmel. He drew an ascent, consisting of six steps. On each step he wrote, "*Nada, nada, nada, nada, nada*"—in English, "nothing, nothing, nothing, nothing, nothing." And even on top of the mountain "*nada*"—"nothing."

Not heavy, not light, not high, not low, not Christian, not Buddhist—just *nada*, or, as Yamada Roshi would say, *"Nani mo nai!"*—"Nothing at all!" And of course for the Buddhists Mount Sumeru is heaven itself!

This is the mountain we must move. If we feel the mountain is beyond our reach, we can cut down the separating distance by throwing away all our concepts of mountains and sit with our Mu of nothingness, sit with the mountain's nothingness. We must not be tempted to despair of its height or weight or kind. And someday, when all things are ready, the gap will suddenly close and, to your great delight, you'll find that the mountain is closer to you than you are to yourself and you can move it easily and freely.

The delights of moving the mountain are manifold. St. John of the Cross scatters them around the top of his mountain as flowers. He calls them peace, joy, happiness, delight, wisdom, justice, fortitude, charity, and piety, and he rounds out his mountain story by quoting the eternal promise of God, "I will bring you into the land of Carmel to eat its fruit and its good things."

The daily training program will reveal itself in many ways. And they will be ways that are personal to you. What will those ways be? I don't know yet.

I am reminded of an experience in the Philippines. At that time, I was traveling to Japan annually for a month or two to deepen my own sitting and experience, and was able to make arrangements for some of our sitters doing advanced koan work to go for a fortnight occasionally, to be exposed to the Roshi's teaching and the aura of San-un Zendo. When they returned to Manila, they had many stories. One man said he caught himself being surprised that the zendo members in Kamakura all had bicycles, the foot-pedal kind. He said he was sure that if they had been Filipinos they would have had powered bicycles!

All through my years of teaching Zen, I have been told many times that one of the reasons people choose to do Zen is to bring some discipline into their lives. Let us tighten up our daily lives so that we're not always just comfortable, but are, rather, "stretching" a little. On the other hand, if we are "over-stretched," just give in a bit to the Inner Source.

Count the number of stars
in the heavens.

6

Whenever I hear this koan, I think of the passage in Genesis 15:5—
"God took Abraham outside and said, 'Look up to the heavens and
count the stars if you can. Such will be your descendants,' he told him.
Abraham put his faith in Yahweh, who counted this as making him
justified."

"Look up to the heavens and count the stars if you can." The koan
from Genesis is the same as in our Zen tradition—with the exception
of the last three words: "if you can." I doubt a Zen master would allow
such an alternative. (But with the mounting air pollution, we might
soon be forced to!)

In any case, we have to count the number of stars in the heavens,
those ancient stepping-stones of Creation.

The Cosmic Walk at the Manresa Retreat Centre in Pickering,
Ontario, sketches the life of stars: the universe began approximately 15
billion years ago, as the primordial flaring forth of stupendous energy
out of ultimate Mystery. The first stars appeared after a billion years,
creating a trillion galaxies, each with billions of stars. 4.6 billion years
ago, our Milky Way galaxy exploded in a flash of brilliance. From the
rich gaseous debris came elements, which will one day become parts of
elephants, Mozart, and us.

One hundred million years later, our star, the sun, is born. Another
one hundred million years later, the earth and the other planets in our
solar system form. Earth is full of fire and creativity. Four billion years
later, bacteria emerge, earth awakens. Life begins.

First we gaze at stars. In 1969, earth was seen from space—the stars gaze at us. Now, sitting in the dokusan room, before the roshi, and under an opaque ceiling (shielding us, most probably, from broad daylight) we have to count into the trillions!

It's enough to make you grateful for the pollution that obliterates a few hundred of the millions of the stars; or even a sudden wind that brings along a blanket of clouds so you couldn't see anything at all. Or maybe you could just run under a table to hide!

"Count the stars in the heavens." The absolute command! A little "can" or "cannot" and body is lost! Life is lost! (To paraphrase Master Mumon in Case 3 of the Gateless Gate.) It's not a case of can or cannot; it's not a case of one star or one million stars; it's not a case of stars and planets. In the world of Zen there's no dichotomy; there is no inside and outside; there is no light and dark. Count the stars in the heavens!

Once when I was interviewing people who wanted to participate in a new series of orientation talks, one young lady described her need as occasioned by a growing tendency to suspicious self-preservation. She described her relation with business associates as one of non-trust...of course in many cases warranted, but still compounded daily. She said, "Even when I receive gifts, I catch myself thinking, 'I wonder what brought that on?' or 'What does she want now?'"

I could not help but think of the grateful openness of a child in receiving a gift—usually with both hands, hugging it to the heart, or better still, trying to swallow it, to be *finally* and *completely* one with it.

Call to a child lying in a crib: the immediate search for eye contact and the quick smile—instantaneous, direct, no conditions! How can we "educate" our children to preserve the purity of that response?

We watch our children discover their first drop of dew sparkling in the sun, or a single solitary snowflake with its geometrical perfection as it falls on a coat sleeve. Their innate sense of awe, reverence, and wonder gladdens our own hearts. If these things bring us joy through our children, why can't they bring us joy directly?

"At that time the Lord exclaimed, 'I bless you Father, Lord of Heaven and Earth, for hiding these things from the learned and the clever, and revealing them to mere children'" (Matthew 11:25–26). What happens to people when they grow up that they can't see "these things" anymore? Perhaps it's because we've become learned and clever! Zen says we are born free, egoless. The Bible says we have this body *(bashar)* and this mind *(nephesh)* and this life-giving Spirit *(ruach)*. This is me!

My education should help me develop these three treasures that are me so that they respond appropriately to all the other treasures, and to "learn" experientially that our life-giving factor, the infinite Spirit, the Empty Infinite, is one and the same with all creation—that we share the same root, as the Zen master tells us.

We all come from the same source; we all receive the same seed. Some seeds fell on the edge of the path, and the birds came and ate them up. Other seeds fell on the patches of rock, where they found little soil and sprang up straightaway because there was no depth of earth. But as soon as the sun came up they were scorched and, not having any roots, they withered away. Others fell among thorns and the thorns grew up and choked them. Others fell on rich soil and produced their crop, some a hundred-fold, some sixty, some thirty. Listen anyone who has ears.

The way we receive the seed, the way we prepare for it and nurture it, may be different among us, but it's the same seed, and we all have it—right from the beginning. If we could realize this experientially, then there would be no Muslim versus non-Muslim problem in the Philippines; there would be no French versus English problem in Canada; there would be no black versus white problem in the United States. Don't you see—*they're all based on illusion.* Essentially, these divisions do not exist! If it weren't so tragic, it could be called stupid.

"Unless you become as little children, you will not enter the Kingdom of Heaven" is as true for Buddhists as it is for Christians. Let us recapture the harmony and integrity we had as children. Let us allow this ego we have built up in our super-intellectual education to melt. Shibayama Roshi says we must die to ourselves so that when we see, we are the seen; when we hear, we are the heard! The only way we can die to ourselves, to bring the ego down to size, is by stopping the intellect from over-extending itself and taking over. C.S. Lewis says simply we must limit the intellect.

Why is it a healing process to limit the intellect? There's a rarely used English word—*bifurcate*—which means to divide into two branches or parts. And whenever it "works," the intellect, by its intrinsic nature, bifurcates. What is in reality *ONE*, it divides into two. This can be seen even in the structure of the languages: English is intellectual, definitive; Japanese isn't. When the Japanese novelist Yasunari Kawabata gave his acceptance speech at the Nobel award ceremony, his talk was entitled *Nihon no utsukushisa no watakushi.* That can't be expressed in English without dividing it into two. In Japanese it means literally "Japan's

Beauty's Me." But since neither the English language nor Western culture will accept that, the title, after many attempts, was changed to
"Beautiful Japan and Me." That which was natural and true and one
in Japanese had to be cut in two in English. The logic of bifurcation
may be great in mathematics, but it is tragic in relationships.

Sitting in zazen puts us in a state of consciousness that does not bifurcate. It strengthens us in the basic unity that is already there. We return
to it as often as possible. We stay in that state of consciousness all
through our day-long sittings, our zazenkai.

In our sitting, whether we are counting our breaths, or saying Mu, or
doing shikantaza, we are taking sure steps in the direction of egoless
harmony. That is why we ask you to persevere in this practice during
your sitting in line for dokusan. And when you enter, and when you
state your koan, don't surface and say, "Good morning, Roshi!" Stay
with your practice until it is time to announce your koan, and state it
quickly and surely. Koans should be memorized.

In the third of Master Tozan's Five Ranks, Yamada Roshi translates
Tozan's verse as, "if concepts have been extinguished completely, then
you may say *anything* as freely as you will...even, for example, if it is
so subtle as to be beyond expression, beyond saying, beyond putting
into words...speak out! And if concepts have been extinguished you
will surpass the eloquence of the most worldly men!"

"The Lord has said, 'Don't be concerned about what you are going
to say, for I will give you the right words and such logic that none of
your opponents will be able to reply.'" (Luke 21:14–15)

Without concepts, our response will be natural, spontaneous, and
instant. I was delighted to learn from the scripture scholar Father H.
Hendricks, CICM, that the famous quotation, "Don't let the left hand
know what the right is doing" means that we must act spontaneously
as indicated by the conditions of the moment, not by a prearranged
program, all thought out by the bifurcating intellect. As Zen would say,
"Do it!"

Now I hesitate to use this phrase "Do it!" because it is being
maligned in many zendos by raw neophytes. When there is not a cloud
to mar the vast sky, we can "Do it!" When we have completely harmonized the bifurcating intellect, we can *DO IT*. In that case it means to
be completely harmonized to the activity of the Essential Nature—
which works like a flash of lightning, never to be caught! *DO IT* is the
fact of God, who has promised that if we don't foul things up with

enormous preparations He will act when the time comes—"Live in me and let me live in you." He is crying out at all times. "Do it!" he said when Peter wanted to walk on the water, and Peter, *without thinking,* instantly and spontaneously jumped over the side of the boat and walked on the water toward the Lord. Then he started to think, to think about walking on the water—and those second thoughts of the intellect gave him fear. And he started to sink! What started as a spontaneous response ended in failure—because of the intellect!

This koan is teaching us to let our Essential Nature respond to the present situation naturally, instantaneously, and spontaneously. Now what have these to do with counting the stars in the heavens?

The journey of a thousand miles starts with a single step.

In a well that has not been dug,
Water is rippling from a spring that does not flow;
There, someone with no shadow or form,
Is drawing the water.

7

Consider the first three words of this koan—"in a well." We immediately conjure in our memory a well we have seen in the past. And even if most of us are city-bred, I daresay we are not unfamiliar with wells. But the well we remember is in the past. Zen has to do with the here and now, so a remembered well cannot be the one we will work with in this koan.

The well in our mind is also a picture. And since there is no reality to a photo, our well here and now is not in our mind, because, dug or not, it cannot hold water. You may have heard of the Zen phrase, "be careful of the third leg of a chicken." If you are hungry, it doesn't matter whether we eat the chicken's left leg or right leg. They both will relieve hunger pangs. But the third leg, the one we only think about, will do nothing to satisfy us.

Usually a well has depth and circumference. But this well has not been dug, so it has no depth or circumference. Can you feel your intellect rejecting that well? Is a well any less a well when it hasn't been dug? Only an undug well is a koan well.

The second line, "Water is rippling from a spring that does not flow." To say a spring does not flow is negating the very meaning of *spring*— issuing forth from the ground is what makes a spring a spring. But with this spring, there is no issuing forth. The water here is from a spring that does not flow from a well that has not been dug. It is too early in our koan study to dwell on No-Mind here. Suffice it to say that enlightened seeing is non-seeing, and knowing is non-knowing.

This rippling water from a spring that does not flow is clearly lacking water indeed. Doesn't the Biblical well come to mind, and the special water our Lord told the woman about?

> The Lord had left Judea and was going back to Galilee. On the way, they came to a well, and being tired and thirsty, they sat down to rest and drink. The apostles were sent to a nearby town to get supplies of food. The Lord, tired by the journey, sat by the well. When a Samaritan woman came to draw water, he said to her, "Give me a drink." She said, "What, you, a Jew, asking me, a Samaritan woman, for a drink?" In fact, they never associated with one another. The Lord replied, "If you only knew what a wonderful gift God has for you, and what I am, you would ask me for some living water." "But you don't have a bucket or a rope," she said, "and this is a very deep well. Where would you get this living water? Are you greater than Jacob, who gave us this well for ourselves and for animals?" The Lord replied that people would soon become thirsty again after drinking this water. "But the water I give them becomes a perpetual spring within them, watering them forever with eternal life." "Please, sir," the woman said, "give me some of that water! Then I'll never be thirsty again and won't have to make this long trip out here every day." (John 4:3–15)

Indeed this water is rippling with life, as the koan tells us. It is living water and whoever drinks it never thirsts again. I don't have to tell you, of course, that there are many tags attached to this living water. But in Zen we do not concern ourselves with the tags, but rather with the taste! It's for a taste of that water that we all come to zazen, and is the whole force of the zendo.

The next line of the koan talks about someone who has come to the well, someone who has no shadow or form. Who is that person? You must sit until you know who that person is. No shadow, no form—as Dogen Zenji said, "Sit until body falls away, until mind falls away." Shibayama Roshi said that you must sit until you die to yourself. A parallel in the Bible is the saying of the Lord, "Anyone who loses his life for my sake will find it." (Matthew 10:39). Will find IT...find what?

The person without shadow or form is drawing living water. Could you get living water by turning on a tap? I beg you not to try for a psychological response. We hear a lot about psychology and Zen these days. Remember, psychology is a new science, and even in its present evolving state, has helped many people, particularly in the West. But it is just in its infancy. I spoke to one psychologist about something she had said that I felt did not apply to the Asian mindset. She very quickly replied, "If you are ever in doubt between anomalies in psychology and Zen, always trust your Zen. It is thousands of years old. We are just starting."

According to some, all mysticism comes under an umbrella called "altered states of consciousness" (ASC), which at times can produce telepathy, clairvoyance, precognition, and even psychokinesis. It is sometimes explained that mystics speak of being "possessed by a spirit," which is more accurately termed "possession by an image." That is to say, the person has within his or her mind an image, which then by an unconscious process takes control of behavior. The psychological term for this process is *dissociation*. The dissociated person experiences this takeover as coming from the outside, in the same way hypnotized people state that they have no control over their limbs. Therefore, the so-called mystic states have been caused or induced by self-hypnosis.

I am in no position to refute or agree with any of the above. All I know is that the Zen experience is the grasping of one's Essential Nature, which is empty. There is no inside or outside, there is no image or agent, and there is nothing for an image to possess. *It* is totally empty and the fact of experiencing this is not self-hypnosis.

The English word *empty* and the Japanese *ku* fit experientially to a degree. Conceptually and emotionally, however, they couldn't be more ill-fitting! Conceptually, to be empty means to lack content—and emotionally it suggests ennui or boredom. Those who have had even the minutest taste of "living water" would wholeheartedly disagree with this understanding.

Ku is loaded! Yamada Roshi suggests "the Empty-Infinite" as an English equivalent; Ruben Habito suggests the Zen circle, which is at the same time the zero/emptiness. The great spiritual masters in both Zen and Christianity speak of the Infinite in negative terms.

Let me tell an old story about the Song of the Bird.

The disciples were full of questions about God.

Said the Master, "God is the Unknown and the Unknowable. Every statement made about Him, every answer to your questions, is a distortion of the Truth."

The disciples were bewildered. "Then why do you speak about Him at all?"

"Why does the bird sing?" said the Master.

A bird does not sing because he has a statement to make. He sings because he has a song.

The words of the scholar are to be understood. The words of the Master are not to be understood. They are to be listened to as one listens to the wind in the trees and the sound of the river and the song of the bird. *They will awaken something within the heart that is beyond all knowledge.*

Let us now reread the koan, with this in mind:

In a well that has not been dug,
Water is rippling from a spring that does not flow;
There, someone with no shadow or form,
Is drawing the water.

Who is that someone with no shadow or form?
How can you show *"ME"* the "Living Water"?

Slowly I wade in a brook
and extinguish its sound.
Freely I watch a flying bird
and sketch the track of its flight.

8

Slowly I wade in a brook...
What a simple, ordinary action, wading in a brook. What are you going to do with this in the dokusan room? Some time ago, someone came to dokusan, said those six words, then closed his eyes, screwed his face up in the most painful expression, and sat there. After two or three minutes, I became alarmed. "What are you doing?" I asked. Never changing his expression or opening his eyes, he said painfully, "I'm wading in the brook!"

The merit of koans is that they compel us in ingenious and often dramatic fashion to learn not simply with our heads, but with our whole being; the spirit of the koan must be demonstrated before the roshi and not explained. "Knowledge is the reward of action; for it is by doing things that one becomes transformed. Executing a symbolical gesture, actually living through to the very limit, a particular role, one comes to realize the truth inherent in the role."[*]

"Executing a symbolic gesture"—slowly I wade in a brook.

"Actually living through to the very limit, a particular role"—slowly I wade in the brook.

Isn't it wonderful!

"One comes to realize the truth inherent in the role." What is the truth inherent in the role of wading in a brook? "No-thought" consists in not attaching oneself to any thought, and in leaving our original (Essential) nature to its natural activity, its original spontaneity

[*]Heinrich Zimmer, *Philosophies of India* (Princeton, NJ: Princeton Univeristy Press, 1969), 544.

67

allowing this nature to be totally itself, pure and spontaneous. I look—the universe is vast and wide. Not a particle to obstruct it.

> *So thick the bamboo grow,*
> *Yet they do not obstruct the running stream;*
> *So lofty the mountain is*
> *Yet it does not impede the white cloud floating.*

Throw away all intellectualization—and plunge into it with your whole being. Unless you present the fact of your own experience, you can never really appreciate what Zen is.

And don't overlook the first word—*slowly.* Let us take our time—let us just take "time"—once in a while. Although sitting is strictly delineated within boundaries of time (three strikes of a bell at the beginning, two at the end) if you are just sitting, and just doing kinhin (walking meditation), and so on, you have passed beyond boundaries. In that condition, there is no "waiting."

Right now—this present moment—is all we have. If we are to be transformed, we simply must see how bounded our present moment is for us. In this year, in this place, we are not tasting vast, limitless space, but rather a squeezed moment, a pressed moment. Do you understand?

Once a man came to dokusan. He said, "If you want to know the truth of it, I sit thirty minutes a day, and spend twenty-five minutes trying to get rid of the thoughts I bring home from work!" I asked him to describe his work. He said that people with big problems come to him, and he has to be continually analyzing what is said and what is not said, and then try to come to a solution. "This is a long process, and I have to keep sorting things out. When I walk to the restaurant to meet another client, I'm still analyzing the last one!"

What kind of Zen practice is that? Where is the call of the bird? If we are to take our Zen practice seriously, I suggest we make our Zen live, and we hear the bird calling us home to our center. That we, several times a day, take three or four minutes to be at home, to just stand up, to just walk to the water fountain, to just let this beautiful water flow over our hands...just this...*just this!*

After a while, the mind will come home very naturally and gratefully. Even a one-breath sit can be very restorative. And all this centering is a preparation for the thirty-minute stretch centering on the cushion.

One of the last calligraphies that Shibayama Roshi made was the lovely Zen saying, "If your heart is peaceful, then every place you go is peaceful."

...and extinguish its sound.

This part of the koan recalls the sounds of nature we spoke about in the first teisho on the temple bell—the sounds that can teach us more about our practice than all the Zen books.

In my notebook, I have made a notation over the word *sound*. It reads, "the call of the nightingale beckons me home." This is a phrase found in the last books we study in the *Shitsunai Shirabe*—the dokusan room study. I paraphrased it, "the call of the bird beckons me home." "Home" is our center, of course, and in our sometimes frenzied lives, we leave home and abandon the spontaneity of our "Essential Action"—Intuitive Action, as one roshi called it.

Sound! A *kyosaku* to return home—our true home—our essential center. The sound of water is one of our loveliest invitations.

You know, the Japanese have a special relationship with water. I do not know the whole cultural background, but body cleanliness is very sacred to them. Their *ofuro,* or honorable bath, is indeed a veritable ritual. Water means so much to them, they feel a need to offer it daily to the Infinite. All of us trainees at the Kamakura Zendo were instructed to change daily the water in the cups on the altars. How do *you* relate to water?

Do not be separate from the sound of water! It is because it is empty that we can become *ONE* in it. Now the verb in the koan is *extinguish*. How can we extinguish something that is empty? That is the point of the koan. How are you going to become one with water?

Freely I watch a flying bird and sketch the track of its flight.

Perhaps we should review what freedom is in Zen. In his *Fukan Zazengi*, Dogen Zenji tells us the principle of Buddhism is complete freedom.

Rinzai Gigen, a Chinese Zen master who died in 866 A.D., wrote:

When I'm hungry, I eat.
When tired, I sleep.
Fools laugh at me.
The wise understand.

Our Essential Nature is free and all-pervading, always wherever we go, wherever we are; it's *right here, right now,* complete, free, and all-pervading. Our life is originally free and unrestricted.

Whenever I come across this koan, I have a vivid memory of seeing a most satisfying presentation of it in Manila some years ago. I had been invited to the home of Lita and Smitty Lanning for dinner. I don't know how it happened, but for a few minutes I was alone in the dining room. Then their little boy Tovey came in to show me his airplane. It was just a small model, no more than a few inches long, but it made no difference to him whether it was ten inches, ten feet, or jumbo-size. That plane swooped and dived and glided with the greatest of ease. It was a most satisfying presentation. I later teased his parents—if only *you* could do as well in the dokusan room!

There was absolutely no separation between Tovey and the airplane. There was, at that moment, absolutely no separation. And I said, with all my heart, "That's a terrific airplane, Tovey!" And I think he understood! Because he was living freely; gut level, mind level, and essential level were all free and living out their oneness with an airplane.

Tovey is going to school now, where his mind level will be developed. Chances are he will start to become less and less proportionately integrated. How tragic that our education, because it's all built on subject and object, stresses separation. For us—you and me—what is it to live freely, body, mind, and essential nature?

Although Zen does not belong in the field of medicine, there are some who practice Zen for bodily health. This is not the way in our zendo, but we certainly respect and benefit from sitting and bodily well-being.

Yamada Roshi treated this subject in his opening comments in an issue of *Kyosho* (a magazine put out by the Sanbo Kyodan):

> Often I speak and write on how our essential self is empty, while at the same time containing wondrous and ultimate capabilities. This is by no means just my personal opinion; I am convinced that this, if we were to sum it up, is the very essence of Zen. This is the world of Zero, which cannot be perceived by our five senses. I do not speak in terms of mere nihilism but rather of emptiness that contains infinite and wonderful capabilities. Among these marvelous capabilities, I believe, is the ability to heal the physical and spiritual disharmonies within us.

It is already common knowledge that the human body possesses natural healing powers. They could also be called natural restorative abilities. Here is a wondrous and wise force contained in our self-nature, in our very life.

And that life is not-two. It is one. Now show *IT* to me as you sketch the track of the bird's flight.

In the sea of Ise, ten thousand feet down,
Lies a single stone;
I wish to pick up that stone
Without wetting my hands.

On the stone a name is inscribed.
What is the name?

On one side of the name it reads,
"Cannot get wet."

On the other side of the name it reads,
"Cannot get dry."

9

If memory serves right, oceanographers tell us that the deepest part of the ocean bed on the earth's surface is the Pacific shelf stretching from Japan past the Philippine Islands. And even if there are places where that ocean bed is just about unfathomable, ten thousand feet down in the Sulu Sea is almost unreachable.

Now, how are you going to get down there? What do you know about deep-sea diving? What do we do when we're faced with a ten-thousand-foot jump into the sea? We know it will be cold and dark, and "unknown." Also, we might as well make up our minds that it's going to take us a quite a long time, in all probability. So we'd better put our 360 bones and joints, and 84,000 pores into it! It's a jump that will cost us something; and once we hit the water, it gets more complicated because in the descent we have to penetrate through layers and layers.

Layers of what? Well, Zen would say layers of ego.

The Bible teaches that we are a monolith born of three dimensions: First, the stuff of the earth and that which relates us to earth—*bashar*—our flesh and blood and bones, our minerals and vitamins. We can feel and pinch and slap. Second, we have a *nephesh* too, which is intellect and will and imagination and memory and feelings, our mind, our spiritual self. Some call this consciousness or soul, which relates us to other people. By themselves, bashar (flesh) and nephesh (soul or spiritual faculties) are lifeless. Third, the Bible tells us that God took the earth and formed man's bashar and nephesh, and then God breathed His breath into man and man became became a *living* being—the *Ruah*—God's breath—our *life*-ing! In the ancient hymn of the Church, "Veni Creator Spiritus," there is a line, "Men, who of thy breathing, move and live." We *move* and *live* because of God's breathing! And if God alone can say "I" then what happens to the basic question, "Who am I?"

Yamada Roshi often said, "I do not know any Christian theology, but I do know that God could create only good things." Hell is man's creation—not God's—and ego is also man's creation. But somewhere, in time and history, dis-harmony entered and we are born without a completely clean slate (and surely the Buddhists mean the original birth when they say we start off perfect). So we soon start to assume the false selves, from our parents, our grandparents, who load us with the expectations of their unfulfilled lives; from our peers, our teachers, television—on and on the layers form. No wonder that legions of young people these days throw up everything the world holds dear and precious (these very layers!) to find out "who I am."

We must also pass through layers of delusion, formed by our bifurcating intellect. Only the intellect could come up with slogans; and concepts like "the superiority of the Aryan race" that justify the slaughter of a whole people. There's no such reality, you know, but nonetheless six million Jews were murdered so that they wouldn't detract from something that doesn't exist! When you look at a Jew, *who* do you see? Well if you don't know who you yourself are, that's a rather stupid question, isn't it?

We are the slogans we see around us today. Test them out yourself. You have probably heard some people say, "I love mankind." But what's a mankind? Show me mankind! You can't because it hasn't a reality. It's just an idea—a concept—a product of the intellect and for intellectual use only. If we're trying to grow, we must do so integrating our whole being, or we're just developing a delusive self.

Under a delusive self, Zen says, greed, anger, and ignorance prosper.

The sea of life has ten thousand layers—at least! And what do we find when we get through these ten thousand layers? The koan tells us: we find a single stone. A single stone! Just one in the vast sea. It is just one, because there is only one! Zen refers to it as the priceless jewel—the Bible calls it the pearl of great price, and extols us to give up everything else to search for that stone. Do you respond to your Zen practice that way?

I would like to share with you a verse by the ancient Chinese thinker, Mencius:

> *When heaven is about to confer*
> *A great office upon a man,*
> *It first exercises his mind with suffering,*
> *And his sinews and bones with toil;*
> *It exposes him to poverty*
> *And confounds all his undertakings.*
> *Then is it seen if he is ready.*

These are crucial days. Perhaps the signs are that we are being made ready for something better. Are you willing to jump ten thousand feet down into the Sulu Sea and pick up that single stone—without getting wet?

As I keep telling you, we must see creation in its two aspects, the phenomenal and the Essential. We are all more or less familiar with the phenomenal aspects, which in the rainy season can become very damp indeed!

To become familiar with the Essential aspect is the business of Zen training. Yamada Roshi, my father in Zen, refers to the Essential Nature as the Empty-Infinite. You probably know that the complete circle, or the zero, is often drawn by Zen masters. There is something complete and perfect about a circle. But it's also empty. (Here, I should add, we're into a language problem. The Japanese call this empty *ku,* which is the *sunyata* of Sanskrit. But in both those languages the emptiness is loaded. In English *empty* means "no content" or "boredom" or "ennui." However experientially the word *empty* fits the reality, emotionally and intellectually it couldn't be more ill-fitting.)

Our Essential Nature is Infinite. But it's empty—it can't be heard, can't be touched, can't be tasted. Once you know this yourself experientially, you'll know how to pick up a stone in the ocean without getting wet at all!

With the permission of the person involved, I'd like to read you the answer of the koan that one of the zendo members wrote to me when I was still in Leyte. He had hesitated in the dokusan room, and I rang the bell for dismissal. "As soon as I walked out of the dokusan room on Sunday, I knew the answer to the koan. It was good that you rang the bell on me so quickly...and...I cannot get wet or dry, or old or young, or sick or well because I am without form. I am not there in shape or form to be affected by anything. I can walk through the Red Sea without getting wet. I can stop a thousand bullets with my hand. I can even go to my office and not get tense. Or at least, I should be able to. Ha! I am an invisible wedge that cuts through anything. Now to live up to that."

The second half of the koan would have us look more closely at that stone. We are told there are three lines inscribed in the shape of an inverted "U":

   1. The top horizontal line is a signature.
   2. The right vertical line reads "Cannot get wet."
   3 The left vertical line reads "Cannot get dry."

Imagine finding an interesting stone like that ten thousand feet deep in the Sulu Sea! Of course people everywhere find interesting stones and coins, and pottery and arrowheads, with all kinds of inscriptions thereon. "This" stone has a signature. *Whose* signature, do you suppose?

The right vertical line reads "Cannot get wet"; that has shades of the first part of the koan. If we find out how we can pick up that stone in the ocean without wetting our hands, we'll know that we cannot get wet.

The left vertical line reads "Cannot get dry." Here I'd like to present a caution, since if you're doing this koan now, it is early in your koan study. As you have often heard, Zen does not deal with opposites. As there is not wet or dry in the Zen world, so there is no presentation of wet and dry as opposites.

This part of the koan does deal with the type of person the Japanese call "wet." Such a person is one who is easily moved to tears. Yamada Roshi says if you cannot weep with a person who is crying, there is no kensho. Zen practice is sensitizing. Realization is our experience of our Essential Oneness with our fellow human beings. Any problem my brother or sister has is my problem. (But I would not have you suspect that Zen promotes an outflow of tears for every hard luck story.)

One of the many definitions of Zen I use (depending on the occasion) is this: "Zen is responding to God's presence at all times, in all circumstances." In Hinunangan, Leyte, when someone from the baybayon (a squatter area along the beach) comes crying to our door for *ulo* medicine (cough medicine) for the sick baby, it is not appropriate at such a time to complain about the unequal distribution of the earth's goods. Children die very quickly in the Philippines. Malnourished to begin with, they soon succumb to the weakening effects of a cold or diarrhea. In such a case, the appropriate response is to grab a thermometer, some aspirin and cough syrup (we make our own) and vitamins, go see the child personally, and then decide whether or not a nurse or doctor should be called.

Buddhism and Christianity are religions of relationships—appropriate relationships. With the mention of Zen, there is often a mistaken idea about the added element of stoicism. In the arena of what I call "secular" Zen, stories abound of the display of unrelenting composure in the face of great danger or personal loss. But oftentimes this is not appropriate.

There is the lovely story of a great woman in Zen whose grandchild died. She was disconsolate. Upon seeing her weeping, some neighbors gossiped. "Her Zen isn't working, see how she cries!" To which the old woman responded, "My grandchild, whom I loved and fed daily, has died. My every tear is a pearl that shines in full brightness."

That reminds me of the sentimental but true story told by Father Edward Flanagan, who in 1917 founded Boy's Town for orphaned boys. He opened the door of his orphanage for boys one night to see a young lad of nine, dirty and obviously exhausted, with a younger boy in the same condition being carried on his back. Father Flanagan said, "All I could think to say was, 'That's a heavy load you have there.'" And the nine-year-old looked up and smiled, "He's not heavy, Father. He's my brother." This is true—or should be true—in all our relationships.

The wet person—sympathetic, easily moved to tears (traits much to be desired)—cannot become dry. A Zen person is one who has come to the realization—if it's true that God is closer to me than I am to myself, then it is true for Ed or Colette or whoever is beside me that as brothers and sisters we are all united, and, with our ensuing compassion, we are deciding daily whether we are going to live as brothers and sisters and not perish as fools (to quote Martin Luther King). That is compassion. It cannot get dry.

With empty hands I take hold of the plow.

While walking, I ride the water buffalo.

As a man crosses the bridge, the bridge flows,
the water remains motionless.

10

With empty hands I take hold of the plow.
As I have said, the English word *emptiness* is an unhappy translation of
the Japanese *ku*—the Sanskrit *shunyata*. Yasutani Roshi defines *ku* as
the *substance* of Buddha Nature: "living," "dynamic," "devoid of
mass," "unfixed," "beyond individuality or personality," "outside the
realm of imagination." It is inconceivable and inscrutable—but we can
nonetheless awaken to it.

You will notice that these are all adjectives, not nouns. An adjective
is open-ended, if you know what I mean. It leads you to the noun it is
describing. "Living," if we want to stop there, is life. It is not appropriate for us in Zen to call *ku* "life" because we have so many preconceived ideas about "life." Capitalizing it—LIFE—helps make clear what
we are trying to grasp, but it still has the smell of other things.

The next word Yasutani Roshi uses is *dynamic,* which connotes activity. The dictionary says, "marked by continuous, usually productive,
activity." If we use the noun-form and translate *ku* as "dynamism," or
"dynamo," we are burdened with the enormous generators we may
have seen, like the huge turbines at the Niagara Falls power plant, or
the almost unimaginable nuclear power centers all over the world today.

The next adjectival phrase "devoid of mass" defines *ku* by what it is
not. To say *ku* is devoid of mass is to say that *ku* has no height, no

depth, no color, no weight, no taste, no smell. Etymologically, the word *devoid* was originally a verb meaning "empty." As a noun *(void)* it means "empty space." To arrive at that empty space, we have to use the "no" steps—no height, no depth, no width, no weight, no color, no size, no taste, no smell, no concept.

We cannot say *ku* is empty, because it is devoid of even the concept of emptiness. We cannot say *ku* is negative because it contains *u*—the "*is*-ness," the Tathagata. Tathagata is non-descriptive, it does not take us "outside" to compare. It simply refers us back to the center in an active-verb kind of way.

Here Christians should feel more at home. Way back in the annals of time, when their religion was in its early formative years, the Jews stormed heaven for God to be revealed—"Who are you?" And the answer they got was "I Am Who Am." The perfect circle; the active verb. And the Yahweh with which we address God is this I Am Who Am—the BEING—a verb.

And so the *ku* is empty—full circle, the Empty-Infinite. Read the koan in that light: "With Empty-Infinite hands, I take hold of the plow."

Look at your hand. Look at it with your third eye. This is what we call the practice of Mu!

While walking, I ride the water buffalo.
Master Daito has a *waka* poem:

> *If you see with your ear and hear with your eye,*
> *Then you will not doubt*
> *These raindrops dripping from the eaves.*

Or again he wrote:

> *Joshu goes with a sandal on his head: Lo!*
> *Three, two, one!*
> *Heaven is earth; earth is heaven.*

Shibayama Roshi calls this the world of reality of Truth, which transcends provincial names and labels, where everything is born anew with creative freedom. I've heard the Yamada Roshi quote in teaching:

The spring breeze in a tree
Has two different faces:
A southward branch looks warm,
A northward branch looks cool.

Equality is at once differentiation. What we have here—walking or riding:

We walk on our feet and
We ride on our backside
Well, which is it?
North or South?
Yes or No?

Another poem the Roshi quotes:

Put grasses together and tie twigs one to another:
Behold here is the cottage!
Dismantle it and take it to pieces:
Behold, it is the original grass field!

One die—many faces: walking? riding?

Of course it is not a question of walking or riding at all because we look at koans from the Essential point of view. I'm not asking how you can ride on a water buffalo while you're walking—or how you can walk while you're riding on a water buffalo. Nor am I asking for an interpretation or conceptual understanding. How can you creatively express Mu here? Your answer must point to the Essential World and transcend both walking and riding.

It goes without saying that you cannot solve this koan by thought. In case you may have forgotten, this might be a good place to review just how we work on koans. First of all, we have to restate the effort of awakening to a direct way of knowing. The first step is to limit the intellect, although it is possible, if you've listened to enough teisho, that you will eventually come to present the koan appropriately to the roshi through an intellectual procedure.

Yamada Roshi teaches us to hang our koan on a hook on the wall. Occasionally (but never while sitting) we let it sift through our consciousness slowly—once—"While walking I ride a water buffalo"—just for a matter of seconds. If nothing comes, then put it back on the hook. A good time to do it is the end of kinhin, as you are readying yourself for another sit.

Even if you cannot give an answer to your koan, it's a good idea to go to dokusan. The roshi may throw a new koan to startle you so that you land in your kensho. Or the worst that can happen is to have the bell rung in your face—but that's an old story now. You will often find that as you leave the room, a response comes to you, and you have to wait until the next dokusan to give it!

"While walking, I ride the water buffalo."

As a man crosses the bridge, the bridge flows...
It seems to me that this koan follows the "Way" of science in trying to understand life. Some years ago, I was fascinated to read *The Tao of Physics* by Fritjof Capra, in which he says that modern physics shows us a view of the world very similar to the views held by the mystics of Asia.

At first glance, it may seem strange that in two totally different areas, one of complex mathematical formalism and the other of mysticism, one finds similar expressions of experiences.

Mystics have always said that ultimately their experience cannot be taught in words. And physicists now join their ranks and adamantly proclaim that their descriptions of reality are limited too, that words are merely representations of reality, like the finger pointing to the moon.

Take a look at the bridge in this koan. "As a man crosses the bridge, the bridge flows." Classical physics would say, "That's ridiculous! Impossible!" because it looks at matter in the way of the Greek atomists—a lot of building blocks, the atoms, which are passive and intrinsically dead, thought to be moved by an external force. This is known as the mechanistic view of physics, which is highly successful as a basis for technology.

"The bridge flows"? Ridiculous! Not without a miracle.

The mystic's view of the world, we are told by Capra, may be characterized by the word *organic* because it regards all phenomena in the universe as integral parts of an inseparable, harmonious whole, and the mystics' view emerges from meditative states of consciousness, attained in non-ordinary experiences. And this organic view of reality becomes extremely useful at the atomic and automatic level, which makes us believe that it is more fundamental than the mechanistic view.

Mystics and modern physics inquire into the essential nature of things in realms that are inaccessible to the ordinary senses. Capra says, "At the beginning of atomic physics, every time the scientists asked nature a question in an atomic experiment, nature answered with a paradox, with the truth hidden in the paradox—not to be proved by logical reasoning, but to be understood in the terms of the new awareness, the awareness of the atomic reality."

What is the atomic reality? As Capra says:

> Far from being the hard and solid particles they were believed to be...atoms turned out to consist of vast regions of empty space in which extremely small particles—the electrons—move around the nucleus....The subatomic units of matter are very abstract entities....Depending on how we look at them, they appear sometimes as particles, sometimes as waves. This leads to the further discovery that, at the subatomic level, matter does not exist. These patterns ultimately do not represent probabilities or interconnections...they have no meaning as isolated entities, but are always interconnected to other things...a complicated web of relations.

Most important, perhaps, the universal interconnectedness of nature always includes the human observer and her or his consciousness. The human observer is not only necessary to observe the properties of an object, but is necessary to define them. We can never speak about nature without, at the same time, speaking about ourselves. Therefore, the human observer becomes the human participator.

Modern physics pictures matter not as inert, but as being in continuous, dancing, and vibrating rhythmic patterns—and the more confined, the faster it moves.

Now, let's take another look at the bridge. Be the human participator!

...the water remains motionless.
In his teisho on Case 14 of the Mumonkan, Shibayama Roshi quotes the koan in one piece:

> *A man passes over the bridge.*
> *Lo! The bridge is flowing and the waters are unmoving.*

The waters are unmoving. We've all had the experience of looking at still water, perhaps water that has been still for so long that it's stagnant.

Yet from the point of view of quantum physics, the subatomic particles are moving at a great rate of speed. But a koan is not physics—it's a living fact!

In Case 24 of the Hekiganroku, Ryutetsuma *went* to Isan. He said, "You old cow, so you've *come*." She said, "There's a party soon at Teisan, are you *going?*"

There's a lot of coming and going in that exchange. What a way for Zen worthies to talk! I think it was Yamada Roshi who calls this *mondo* a *Buppo*-battle, a dharma combat to make roads (for coming and going) where there aren't any!

In the Zazen Wasan ("Song of Zazen"), we chant, "coming and going, never astray" or, as another translation has it, "there is no coming or going, and yet by always moving to and fro, one is always still." That's nonsense enough to be a koan indeed!

There's a lovely "song" by the poet John Donne, "Go and catch a falling star." It's second verse reads:

> *If thou be'st born to strange sights,*
> *Things invisible to see,*
> *Ride ten thousand days and nights,*
> *Til age snow white hairs on thee.*

You must ride ten thousand days and nights, until your hair has turned white, to see things invisible. Zen tells us if there is as much as a paper-thin distance between us and "things invisible," they might as well be ten thousand miles away. *Where* are things invisible to see? *Where* is Ryutetsuma's Taisan? If we think we have to go somewhere, we are very green indeed!

This koan is telling us the water is motionless. It is saying that all your coming and going takes place now—here, where you are.

As you well know, we view our koans from the Essential aspect. It is of utmost importance that we experience our own Essential Nature—and to experience that our own Essential Nature and that of the universe is One. There is no time or place where this is not so. There is no coming or going.

The water is motionless.

How will you show me in the dokusan room that your Essential Nature and the Essential Nature of the water are one? A living fact!

In order to be worthy as a Zen student,
I must go straight on a narrow mountain road
That has ninety-nine curves.

11

For some reason or other, when I read this koan, I think of a natural phenomenon at my birthplace in Moncton, New Brunswick, in eastern Canada. There is, just outside the city, a place called Magnetic Hill. As you approach the spot, a large billboard gives the instruction to drive down the hill from that spot. Note that you have to press on the accelerator more as you approach the foot of the hill. When you get there, stop; put the car in neutral; and the car will coast back up the hill, moving faster as it approaches the top. At which point there is a mad scramble to keep out of the way of other drivers gone berserk, who just can't believe what is happening. You can always see people getting out of their cars and checking to look, yes, the water in the ditch *is* rolling up the hill; and you can plainly see that the tops of the telephone poles down at the foot are lower than your vantage point at the top of the hill. Local people will wink and explain "Our hill's magnetic!" (Whatever that means!) Back in town, they will smile at that explanation and tell you it's an optical illusion.

It is probably the "optical illusion" reference that reminds me of the koan, a narrow mountain road that has ninety-nine curves. I daresay there isn't one person in our zendo who wouldn't immediately grasp the possible Zen barrier of those ninety-nine curves! What are you going to do with one curve in the dokusan room?

In the first of the orientation talks, everyone receives a "practice" and from then on, as long as you are an active member of the zendo, you have a "practice." We think of it primarily as what we are doing while we are on our cushion. For instance, people will come to doku-san and say, "I'm practicing Mu." I ask you to remember that our Zen practice doesn't stop on the cushion. But it's not that we do Mu all day long. We do not walk down the street with our eyes half-closed saying *Mu!* We could easily be hit by a car if we did that! In Zen, our practice is what we are doing now. When we eat, we eat; when we work, we work. As Zen practitioners, we say, at mealtime, our practice is eating; and at *samu*, our practice is work. In some temples samu is called work-practice. And the appropriateness of doing our practice is covered in the Japanese word *tada*, which means "only" or "just." Just eating. Just working.

I'd like to tell you how dishes are washed in the Philippines. First we scrape off the food particles from the plate and rinse it with a little water, which in turn is put in a receptacle for one of the domesticated animals. The dishes are then taken to the sink where they are soaped well. Then they are rinsed and put on a rack where they are dried, to be taken eventually to the cupboard and stacked neatly. In each of these actions, we do *only* that, we do *just* that; we *just soap* the dishes, we *just rinse* the plates, etc. Being one with our present activity is central to Zen practice.

The deeper the realization of our fundamental oneness, the more our practice becomes authentic and transparent, the less the "I" becomes. When we wash dishes as though we don't want to wash dishes, our aggressive ego is strengthened. When you recognize that egoless sitting in zazen is helpful, then you will soon realize that egoless dishwashing is also helpful.

In my own life, I frequently try to check on my relationships, espe-cially toward people with whom I am living. It has been said we are often hardest on our spouse and on our own family. Of course we know that the more distant a relationship, the easier it is to be harmonious and understanding. It's a good measuring rod to check on the pronoun-subject of my sentences. If it is frequently "I," the rest may not be in harmony with my practice. When it starts with "he" or "she," things seem to be improving.

Our Zen practice does not start and end on our cushion. Each day should be twenty-four hours of harmonious practice. Whether we look after a family, wash dishes, drive a truck, teach school, or work in a barrio, we are focused and at *one*. And although we make sitting with the sangha a priority we gradually realize that our wider community is all beings everywhere. Gradually the hard boundaries that separate us from the rest of the world will soften. In our busy world today, we easily become afflicted with separateness, which is the disease of the century. Granted, there are many differences between a modern sangha, each member of which is already over-extended, and a rural monastery of Buddhist monks living a schedule designed for sitting and its consequences. But let us not forget that if there are no consequences to our sitting, then we might as well close shop, as the saying goes.

According to one Buddhist story, there are many similarities between heaven and hell. One day an eminent teacher took her students to a far-off building, which was marked "Heaven and Hell." They went in through the large front door, and saw immediately, that the building contained only two rooms, one marked "Hell" and the other "Heaven." The teacher went up to the door of Hell, opened it, and her disciples saw a huge room filled with large tables, on which were heaped lots and lots of delicious-looking food. But the thousands of people there were roaring with anger, hunger, and pain because the chopsticks were five feet long and they could not get the food into their mouths. The teacher and her group left Hell and went to the door of Heaven, and the minute they opened the door, they were surprised to see that here too was a large room with many tables loaded with all kinds of delicious-looking food. But everyone was happy and well fed. Oh yes, the chopsticks were also five feet long, but the people used them to feed, not themselves, but those opposite them at the table. It was a scene of perfect contentment.

Now to get back to the mountain with ninety-nine curves. We are going up the mountain path single-mindedly. I'll repeat that. We are going up the mountain single-mindedly. What is this mind that is single? One step at a time. The mind is the agent controlling the tired feet, one winding step after the other. The mind is also the gateway, as Master Mumon tells us, to our Essential Nature, which is right down to the tips of our toes! With every step, countless buddhas come forth from our toes, Left! Right! Left! Right! Just one step after another.

We know that we must view every koan from the Essential point of view. How are our "empty" feet doing on the curves? They have only one way to go! *Straight as a die!* There are no curves in the Essential road...we go straight on a mountain path that has ninety-nine curves. No optical illusion here! Can you do it?

The leaves of the lotus are round, round,
Rounder than a mirror.

The edge of the water-nut is sharp, sharp,
Sharper than an awl.

When the wind blows through the willows,
The downy seed-balls float away.

When the rain beats on the pear blossoms,
A butterfly flies away.

12

The leaves of the lotus are round, round, rounder than a mirror.
This koan has to do with leaves. How do you *feel* about leaves? I am
not sure what leaves mean to everyone, but I know very well what
leaves means to North Americans, for whom the four seasons are
clearly delineated.

Leaves are the harbingers of the seasons for us. In late February and
early March, when snow piles have collected pollution and soot, and
the weariness of winter becomes burdensome, the heart is gladdened
by the promise of spring, in the little nodes that are forming on the
branches that have been barren for months. And as the snow piles lessen
and we begin to discard our many layers of winter clothes, we watch the
tiny swellings on the trees break open, and the tender green shoots peek
out—but not too quickly, because the nights are still cold. Every day,
each sprout shows a little more of itself, and should there even be
another late snow, the hope of new life is there for us to see. The leaves
fill out with the rains of early spring.

In summer, the large mature leaves shade us from the harmful rays of the sun, and in autumn, when the sun's heat wanes, the leaves seem to know their work is done. Their farewell in Canada is one of the wonders of the world, I believe. The Japanese are one with leaves. All traditional Japanese culture comes under the umbrella of *shibui,* the refined subdued shades of their autumn colors.

As far as leaves are concerned, most cultures are one with nature. When their colors fade to somber brown, something inside our hearts fades too, as we reach for a sweater against the autumn chill. North American literature is filled with references to fallen leaves. And one of my own favorite personal memories is walking with a friend through a field of fallen leaves, with hands jammed in the pockets of a cozy sweater.

The American poet Robert Frost, who wrote in New England, not too many miles from where I was born and grew up, finds in leaves a whole philosophy of life...

In Hardwood Groves

The same leaves over and over again!
They fall from giving shade above
To make one texture of faded brown
And fit the earth like a leather glove.

Before the leaves can mount again
To fill the trees with another shade,
They must go down past things coming up.
They must go down into the dark decayed.

They must be pierced by flowers and put
Beneath the feet of dancing flowers,
However it is in some other world
I know that this is the way in ours.

Perhaps when you work on this koan, leaves will come to shape your philosophy of life. In this koan, we do not deal with leaves in general, but with one specific leaf, namely a lotus leaf. A lotus is very significant in Zen. Most of the pictures and statues of Shakyamuni have him sitting on a lotus leaf.

In this koan, the leaf of the lotus is round, round, rounder than a mirror. Do you get the feel of that? Round, round, round. Some rounds are very round indeed, and this is especially true of a Japanese mirror. Perhaps one of the reasons a Japanese mirror is round is because it has a dimension of depth. For instance, a mirror framed by the famous *kibori* artists in Kamakura is set in a frame so that the wood is at right angles to the mirror, and that depth makes the mirror seem very round.

G.K. Chesterton tells us that we must look at ordinary things until they become extra-ordinary. In Zen, we must see not only with our two eyes. Listen to this quotation from Elizabeth Barrett Browning:

> *Earth's crammed with heaven,*
> *And every common bush afire with God;*
> *And only he who sees takes off his shoes;*
> *The rest sit round it and pluck blackberries.*

We do not gather blackberries in the zendo. We just hope to *see*. The leaves of the lotus are round, round, rounder than a mirror. The mirror-like enlightened mind we read about in Buddhist texts sees a well-polished transparent mirror of whatever size, reflecting everything totally. A round lotus leaf totally; nothing left over. How does your fully polished transparent mirror-like enlightened mind reflect a round, round lotus leaf that is rounder than a mirror?

Yamada Roshi used to say there are many round things in everyday life: there are round sounds in music; the sweet taste in food is round; also fondling the head of a child is round—I have seen him do this with Junko, his little granddaughter. He would put her on his knee and gently rub her head with the palm of his hand, round and round and round.

The edge of the water-nut is sharp, sharp, sharper than an awl.

The center part of the water-nut is round, something like a chestnut, and the two ends are pulled out to very sharp points. Since I have never seen one, I do not feel any affinity to a water-nut. But I am very familiar with an awl, the other phenomenon mentioned in the koan. I'm sure you know it is a pointed instrument, about the shape and size of an ordinary pencil. Its very sharp tip is used for marking surfaces or piercing small holes in leather or wood. All carving artists have awls.

With both the water-nut and the awl, we are confronted with sharpness. If I may pun on it, that is the "point" of this koan. And whenever I think of sharpness, I think of a story by Chuang Tsu.

> Prince Wen Hui's cook was carving up an ox. Every touch of his hand, every heave of his shoulder, every step of his foot, every thrust of his knee, with the slicing and parting of the flesh, and the swinging of the knife, all was in perfect rhythm, just like the Dance of the Mulberry Grove. Prince Wen Hui remarked, "How wonderfully you have mastered your art."
>
> The cook laid down his knife and said, "What your servant really cares for is Tao, which goes beyond mere art. When I first began to cut up oxen, I saw nothing but oxen. After three years of practicing, I no longer saw the ox as a whole. I now work with my spirit, not with my eyes. My senses stop functioning and my spirit takes over. I follow the natural grain, letting the knife find its way through the many hidden openings, taking advantage of what is there, never touching a ligament or tendon, much less a main joint.
>
> "A good cook changes his knife once a year because he cuts, while a mediocre cook has to change his every month because he hacks. I've had this knife of mine for nineteen years and have cut up thousands of oxen with it, and yet the edge is as if it were fresh from the grindstone. There are spaces between the joints. The blade of the knife has no thickness. That which has no thickness has plenty of room to pass through these spaces. Therefore, after nineteen years, my blade is as sharp as ever. However, when I come to a difficulty, I size up the joint, look carefully, keep my eyes on what I am doing, and work slowly. Then with a very slight movement of the knife, I cut the whole ox wide open. It falls apart, like a clod of earth crumbling to the ground. I stand there with the knife in my hand, looking about me with a feeling of accomplishment and delight. Then I wipe the knife clean and put it away."
>
> "Well done!" said the Prince. "From the words of my cook, I have learned the secret of growth."

This man was truly a "sharp cook"!

The edge of the water-nut is sharp, sharp, sharper than an awl. The awl is the same as the cook's knife. But so is paper also sharp. Have you ever cut yourself with the edge of a piece of paper? Sharp suggests something to me that is breathing, alive, provocative like an awl or a butcher's knife. And there are many sharp things in everyday life: an accent in music, a sharp reply, a sharp taste like Indian curry.

But these are all words. Use the awl as a skewer and run it through you and the edge of the water-nut. Show me what is the sharpest— quickly, no hesitation or delay!

**When the wind blows through the willows,
the downy seed-balls float away.**
Many Asians, particularly the Japanese, think the origin and source of the wind is right in the Philippines. When I lived in Japan, it was frequently stated on the *Tenki Yoho* (the weather forecast) that typhoons which yearly roar through the country during late August and September generate in the Samar-Leyte region of the Philippines. Where I lived on the floor of the provincialate on Aurora Boulevard, there was almost always a lovely breeze blowing. I think Filipinos are very intimate with winds.

You know what happens when the wind blows. Things move; things well rooted just move back and forth. Most breezes have a kind of caressing touch. Have you ever noticed how the wind moves things? Treat yourself to watching the wind at the next outside kinhin. Generally speaking, the wind seems to have a kind of fluid quality. It moves through and around round things.

This is quite different from the way things usually move. We tend to push and pull, don't we? Things are objects; we're here, they're there; we pull them here, or push them there. That's what happens when we objectify things. And the acts of pulling and pushing are the beginnings of violence.

The wind passes through a tree, seems to find itself there, and carries on, leaving the tree where it is, refreshed and having been experienced. Not a wonder the Holy Spirit came as a wind. The flow of the wind is a part of the flow of the great unifying dynamism, the flow of energy, the flow of things, the cosmic flow, which is in motion throughout the universe.

In the practice of Zen we must move every day, every instant, quite naturally, according to that flow. As Yamada Roshi says, "All our actions should be as ordinary as the flow of water. To go against the stream is not the way of Zen."

I can tell you quite frankly that that is not the ambience of my upbringing in Canada. Not too many generations back, our pioneers were immobilized in cold isolation for six months of the year, unable to get to their neighbors during the worst of the winter months, living on stored, dried, or preserved foods, melting snow for drinking water. Canadians are descendants of "rugged individuals." No other type could survive our severe climate.

In high school I well remember one of our most respected teacher's call to arms: "any old fish can float downstream—it takes a *live* one to swim against the current." Because that is *my* background, I have to be especially careful to allow the wind to take the down-willow seed where it will. We all have to ask ourselves how our culture and history condition our response to the flow of life itself.

We can live more easily, you know, when we can recognize the flow. First, we must realize the flow is already in motion. We should help the flow along in our daily life. Here again, as in zazen, concepts are not helpful, because they are static, pictures in our head, not in the flow. So beware of giving advice that is based on a concept. Indeed, beware of all advice because our advice is where *we're* at. We must not only listen to people, we must hear them out where they are, hear what's happening, and help it to happen.

It's in this line of happening that I keep talking about the evolving of our zendo and real authentic Zen. We are involved in a growing experiment that's in flow, that's going somewhere (so to speak), a kind of evolving organism. You and I must keep an open mind. Let the flow happen, help it along. It will come to its appropriate fulfillment to the extent that we, again you and I, can let go of preconceived ideas about the way it should be, or the way it is supposed to be. Our ideas should be fluid and move with the wind. People with fixed notions are usually standing still.

If one of the issues of *Ten Directions,* it is recorded that someone asked Bernie Glassman, "Roshi tells us to give people what they want, rather than what we think they need." In part, Glassman answered, "Someone comes asking for something, because the flow is already in motion, and there are, in fact, things that they want to do. For example, people who say, 'I want to commit suicide' are probably saying, 'I want to lead a good life'...now you can't make me lead a good life, but you can somehow stick out a leg, so that I trip in that direction. What is tricky is that the word and the act which is what is really going on can delude us."

"What is really going on?" Glassman says. Surely that is the matter of our daily life. And never let us forget in our koan study, that if we don't put to use what we learn here, it becomes just so much garbage.

To be in the flow of what is really going on gives our awareness flow. An American Jesuit has spent many years in Thailand, and the problem he experiences when he goes to the Buddhist monasteries there that bothers him most is the practice of awareness in a kind of slow motion. He said they will do what we call kinhin, taking one step every ten minutes, or drink water, using twenty minutes to get your hand to the cup. "It drives me bugs," he said.

On the one hand, we can see the goal that kind of training is getting at. On the other hand, we can also understand the American's frustration. I tried my own awareness in taking a step and grasping a cup of water. I never realized before how strong the *flow* of awareness, the *flow* of attention, really is in our practice.

Now to get on with the flow of our koan. "When the wind blows through the willows, the downy seed-balls float away." It's a Chinese willow, and the size is fairly large—perhaps like the blue willow pattern so often seen on Chinese dishes. The seed must be fairly large—it moves sideways as if it floats, much the same movement as when we respond to a voice calling from beside us.

Anyway, the seed is downy, and it floats with the wind. Oh that we could be a downy seed-ball, with no concepts, no preconceived ideas or fixed motions, and be carried where the wind would have us go!

When the rain beats on the pear blossoms, a butterfly flies away.
This koan also reminds me of Chuang Tsu. In the same book I quoted above, we read the following:

> Once upon a time, I, Chuang Tsu, dreamed I was a butterfly, flying happily here and there, enjoying life without knowing who I was. Suddenly I woke up and I was indeed Chuang Tsu. Did Chuang Tsu dream he was a butterfly, or did the butterfly dream he was Chuang Tsu?"

Basho wrote a haiku on this:

You are a butterfly
And I the dreaming heart
Of Chuang Tsu.

Robert Aitken Roshi tells us the occasion of this haiku was a kind "thank you" note that Basho sent to a friend, Doi by name, who had given him a writing brush. In *A Zen Wave*, Aitken Roshi says:

> As he often did, Basho took inspiration from old writings and turned the entire idea completely about to make a new and fresh poem. While Chuang Tsu was playing with interpenetration and transformation of all things, but specifically himself and a butterfly, Basho was playing with his friend, personalizing the sangha.
>
> Basho, the adult child who had long since entered the kingdom of heaven, said "You're the butterfly, and I the dreaming heart of Chuang Tsu. I don't know if I'm Basho who dreamed with the heart-mind of Chuang Tsu that I was a butterfly named Doi, or that winged Mr. Doi was dreaming he is Basho." How intimate. How happy his friend must have been.
>
> As Chuang Tsu himself says: "Someday there will be a great awakening when we know that this is all a great dream. Yet the stupid believe they are awake, busily and brightly assuming they understand things, calling this man ruler, that one herdsman—how dense!"

The secret in Zen is not to think, not to assume, but *to be*. The purpose is not to *mean* something, but to present something. Don't come to dokusan with this koan and tell me you are one with the butterfly. As Aitken Roshi says, "If Chuang Tsu had said, 'The butterfly and I are one,' he would have expired on the spot, and nobody would have remembered him for longer than a week. If Basho had said, 'I'm you and you are I,' his friend Doi would have demanded his brush back."

Once upon a time, I dreamed I was a butterfly, flying happily here and there, enjoying without knowing who I was. Suddenly I woke up, and I was indeed myself.

Did I dream I was the butterfly, or did the butterfly dream it was I?

When the rain beats on the pear blossoms, a butterfly flies up.

On Mount Godai
A cloud is cooking rice.

In front of an old Buddhist shrine
A dog is pissing toward heaven.

13

This commentary will address only the first part of this koan. In this koan, we find that on Mount Godai (wherever that is) a cloud is cooking rice. Now that's a funny thing for a cloud to do, isn't it! This koan came to life for me when I once flew to Manila from Cebu. There were many clouds in the sky, great cumulus clouds. From a distance, they looked like chunks of clouds, but once we got into them, they seemed to go on and on—there were no comforting glimpses of the earth and city at all—nothing but clouds, in front, behind, on top, and underneath. Even the airplane seemed full of clouds, and gradually my 360 bones and joints and 84,000 pores were full of clouds. And then I laughed, "This cloud can cook rice—this cloud can write a letter—this cloud can go to the comfort room."

Do you know a cloud that cooks rice? Be careful you do not fall into the trap of making distinctions between clouds that can, and clouds that can't.

There is a Zen story:

> As Seigun entered the temple, he noticed a sparrow making droppings on an image of the Buddha, and said to Nyoe, "Has the sparrow Buddha Nature or not?"
> Nyoe answered, "Yes."

Seigun said, "Then why does it make droppings on the head of the Buddha?"

Nyoe replied, "Does it make droppings on the head of a hawk?"

What is Nyoe saying? Is he saying the head of a hawk is different from the head of the Buddha? This is the world of distinctions as grasped by our intellect. There is another world of no distinctions, which has been graphically illustrated by a contemporary Zen master in the following illustration:

> In a cookie factory, different cookies are baked in the shape of animals, cars, people and airplanes. They have different names and forms, but they are all made from the same dough, and they all taste the same.

In the same way, all things in the universe—the sun, the moon, the stars, the mountains, rivers, people, and so forth—have different names and forms, but they are all made from the same substance. The phenomenal universe is organized into pairs of opposites: light and darkness, man and woman, sound and silence, good and bad. But all these opposites are made from the same substance. Their names and their forms are different, but their substance is the same. Names and forms are made by thinking. If you are "not thinking" and have no attachment to name and form, then all substance is one. And this is the world where there are no distinctions.

We must not imagine that sitting with our "not thinking" mind is suppressing all thoughts. Eno, the sixth patriarch, in his teaching insists on the fact that absence-of-thought does not mean suppression of thinking, but being free of all thought. He reproaches certain teachers for "forming logs" instead of disciples by imposing on them the stupefying exercise of suppressing thoughts (which is destined to failure). "Not producing thoughts" or, no-thought, consists in not *attaching oneself* to any thought, and leaving our Essential Nature to its natural activity, its own spontaneity.

In other words, thoughts produce objects. Thoughts are the cookie-cutters that make people and animals and houses and trees and buddhas and hawks and mountains and clouds and rice that has to be cooked.

The phrase "attachment thinking" may not be clear. For example, if you drive a car with attachment thinking, your mind will be somewhere else and you will, perhaps, go through a red light. *No-attachment* thinking means that your mind is clear all the time, just like the mirror I so often mention in teaching. When you drive, you aren't thinking, you are just driving. One Zen teacher has called it intuitive action. Intuitive action means acting without any desire or attachment. To illustrate, we can return to the Buddhist mirror. "My mind is like a clear mirror, reflecting everything, just as it is. Red comes and the mirror becomes red. *STOP!* Sadness comes, and the mirror becomes sad. *TEARS!* That is how a bodhisattva lives. No selfish desires; actions all for people."

Have you ever seen Yamada Roshi take his *kotsu* (teaching stick) and teach Zen by means of a circle? He starts in the upright position, and he explains as he moves it along to the 90-degree area, that through this period we have much thinking and many desires. Thinking can bring desire and desire is suffering. In this arc, all things are separated into objects and opposites: good and bad, yours and mine, beautiful and ugly. I like this, I don't like that. I try to get happiness and avoid sufferings.

Then after 90 degrees we get some insight. Before you were born you were 0, now you are 1; after you die you'll become 0 again. So 0 = 1 = 0.

This is the same for all, so in this arc, we see all things as the same because they have the same substance. All things have name and form, but their names and forms come from emptiness and will return to emptiness. Still lots of thinking in this area, but in our focused practice, we keep going back to the zero—back home. We put on clothes of emptiness, we speak without moving our lips, and we walk straight on a mountain path that has ninety-nine curves.

Then we move to 180 degrees—and there the Roshi will pretend his stick is a bit stuck, and he gives it a special little push, which he calls the experience of true emptiness. It is before thinking, before cookie-cutting, and there are no words and no speech. There are no mountains, no people, no trees, and no houses. There is only...*kachin!* But if you stay at 180 degrees, you become attached to emptiness.

The next area is 270 degrees. Here is complete freedom. A cloud can cook rice on Mount Godai. I can move Mount Mayon. I can ring the temple bells in Japan. I can put out a fire one thousand miles away. Committing and negating are interfusing; buddhas and ancestors have to beg for their lives. Shibayama Roshi called this area "rebirth," a barrier that has to be broken through, or we cannot be really free in living our actual everyday lives.

One of the loveliest stories of this arc portion is told by Seung Sahn, a Korean Zen master who taught extensively in America. (He also gave us the cookie dough analogy I mentioned previously.)

> One evening, Katz, a black cat with a white-tipped tail, who lived at the Cambrage Zen Center, died after a long illness. The seven-year-old daughter of one of Seung Sahn's students was troubled by the death. After the burial and chanting to Amida Buddha, she went to Seung Sahn for an interview.
>
> Seung Sahn said, "Do you have any questions?"
>
> Gita said, "Yes. What happened to Katzie? Where did he go?"
>
> Seung Sahn said, "Where do you come from?"
>
> "I come from my mother's stomach."
>
> "Where does your mother come from?"
>
> Gita was silent.
>
> Seung Sahn said: "Everything in the world comes from the same one thing. What are they? There are no words. A cat doesn't say 'My name is sun.' It is just a cat. So when someone asks you 'What is this?' how should you answer?"
>
> "I shouldn't use words."
>
> Seung Sahn said, "Very good! You shouldn't use words. So if someone asks you, 'What is Buddha?' what would be a good answer?"
>
> Gita was silent.
>
> Seung Sahn said, "Now you ask me."
>
> "What is Buddha?"
>
> Seung Sahn hit the floor.
>
> Gita laughed.
>
> Seung Sahn said, "Now I ask you: What is Buddha?"
>
> Gita hit the floor.
>
> "What is your mother?
>
> Gita hit the floor.
>
> "What are you?"
>
> Gita hit the floor.
>
> "Very good! This is what all things in the world are made of. You and Buddha and your mother and the whole world are the same."

Gita smiled.

Seung Sahn said, "Do you have any more questions?"

The little girl said, "You still haven't told me where Katz went."

Seung Sahn leaned over, looked into her eyes, and said, "You already understand."

Gita said, "Oh," and hit the floor very hard. Then she laughed.

Seung Sahn said, "Very good! That is how you should answer any question. That is the truth."

Gita bowed and left.

As she was opening the door, she turned to Seung Sahn and said, "But I'm not going to answer that way when I'm in school. I'm going to give the regular answer."

Seung Sahn laughed.

270 degrees, the area of freedom. If you stay there, you become attached to freedom.

The last arc is 360 degrees—back to zero—we arrive where we began, where we have always been. But there is all the difference in the world between a person who has passed through the cycle, the process, and one who has remained stuck at zero. 360 degrees, things are just what they are: mountains are mountains and rivers are rivers. There is no attachment, there is no attachment thinking. And I quote one more time, T.S. Eliot's words:

> *And the end of all our exploring*
> *Will be to arrive where we started*
> *And know the place for the first time.*

Now a last point, which is of utmost importance: At 360 degrees, the circle disappears. The circle is just an expedient. It does not exist at all. As we hear in the Third Ancestor's poem "Trust in Mind":

> *The Great Way is not difficult*
> *If you do not make distinctions.*
> *Only throw away likes and dislikes*
> *And everything will be perfectly clear.*

You will say, "But that circle-teaching-Zen uses distinctions." You are right. All words are distinctions. But remember it is you who make the distinctions. You make the differences; it is not the words. If you are attached to words, you cannot return to your essential center. If you are "thinking," any words are unacceptable.

But if you are "not-thinking," all words and all things that you can see or hear or smell or taste or touch will help you. That is why we have outdoor kinhin, after periods of "no-thinking" sitting.

Master Lin Chi said, "Inside a wall of pink flesh, lives the Utmost Master. All day long, this Master goes in and out through the six doors."

Treat yourself occasionally to an out-of-doors kinhin. All things are teaching you at every moment and nature sounds are better teaching than all the books "about" Zen.

There is a story about Su Tung-po, which parallels Tokusan. Su Tung-po was one of the greatest poets in the Sung dynasty. He was famous not only as a poet, but as an essayist, a painter, and a calligrapher as well. From an early age, he studied the Confucian and Buddhist classics. It is said he knew the entire Buddhist canon of 84,000 volumes by heart. His hobby seems to have been examining the Zen masters and monks of his era.

One day, Su Tung-po was told that in a nearby monastery there lived a very learned Zen master, who would certainly be able to answer any question he could ask. So he mounted his horse and rode off to see for himself. Traditionally, a visitor waits at the monastery door to be escorted inside. But Su Tung-po opened the door himself, rode in, went directly to the main lecture hall, and sat down with his back to the Buddha.

When the Master entered, he bowed respectfully to Su Tung-po and said, "We are honored by your presence, sir. Welcome. What, may I ask, is your name?"

"My name is Ch'eng." [*Ch'eng* means "scales"]

"Mr. Scales? What a curious name!"

"I am called that because I can weigh all the eminent teachers in the land."

At once, the Master let out an ear-splitting yell. Then with a faint smile, he said, "How much does that weigh?" The answer to this was in none of the sutras and our Su Tung-po was speechless. His arrogance crumbled—he bowed to the Master, and began to devote himself to Zen.

Sometime later, he determined to visit another master he had heard about and asked, "Please teach me the Buddha dharma and open up my ignorant eyes."

The Master, whom he had expected to be the very soul of compassion, begun to shout at him, "How dare you come here seeking the dead words of men! Why don't you open your ears to the living words of nature! I can't talk to someone who knows so much about Zen. Go away!"

What was the teaching that nature could give and words could not? Totally absorbed in this question, Su Tung-po mounted his horse and rode off. He lost all sense of direction, so he let his horse find the way. It led him on a mountain path. Suddenly he came to a waterfall. The sound struck his ears and they were opened. He came to enlightenment. He was one with the whole universe. He got off his horse and bowed to the ground in the direction of the monastery.

That evening he wrote the following poem:

The roaring waterfall
is the Buddha's golden mouth.
The mountains in the distance
are his pure luminous body.
How many thousands of poems
have flowed through me tonight!
And tomorrow I won't be able
to repeat even one word.

If the mountains in the poem are the Buddha's pure luminous body, why can't the cloud on the mountain cook rice?

A thousand mountains are covered with snow.

Why is only one peak not white?

14

In this commentary, I will blend the two parts of this koan together in presentation: the many—the one.

I used to wonder, when I taught in the Philippines, as we sat in the tropical heat mopping our brows, how we could become one with this koan of mountains covered with snow. Some sangha members had never experienced snow. As a Canadian, I related that I'd had some very happy and not so happy snow experiences.

New fallen snow is beautiful for only two or three days. It gradually forms a crust and pollution from the air dirties it. And then there's another snowfall and a shiny whiteness that is exceedingly soft! Have you ever given a thought about the experience of being in the middle of falling snow? Each little snowflake is a thing of great beauty, geometrically perfect. Snowflakes remind me of the shapes that appear in a kaleidoscope as we rotate it. Each shape is symmetrical and intricately designed with several protruding parts. These parts interlock easily with other snowflakes, so they are prone to adhere and pile up. Even just walking to a bus stop, you can acquire a fair amount of piled-up snow on your hat and the shoulders of your coat. Before you get into a warm bus, you always brush off what has collected in these two areas.

Now let's look at the koan again. Line one tells us that we have a thousand mountains. I'm sure you have become familiar enough with your Zen studies to know that "a thousand" is pointing to the phenomenal world. Line two deals with the number one, and with not-white. So: What world has no color?

Here is the classical presentation of a koan, and it would be interesting to enumerate the koans we have in our *Shitsunai Shirabe* (dokusan studies) concerning mountains. In one sense, Mount Fuji is the spiritual home for all koans for the Japanese. Perhaps one day we'll go to the Rocky Mountains for sesshin and adopt one of the peaks as our spiritual home.

While in Japan, I did some work with a television company on the life of the famous artist, Hokusai. He drew a set of pictures concerning Mount Fuji, and there must be easily one hundred pictures in the lot. Mount Fuji has many faces. And in one of Hokusai's sketchbooks there is a picture of an artist in a frenzy of drawing with five brushes at the same time. He is lying on his back with a brush in each foot, each hand, and a fifth one in his mouth. He is desperately engaged in painting. It is like the thousand mountains. The artist with five brushes is depicting the phenomenal world!

I'd like to spend a little time with the artists who depict the Essential World. We have been considering a logo for our zendo. It has to communicate the Essence to us. Our artist, Stan Krzyzanowski, whose design we chose, has endeavored to keep it from looking solid, and also to keep it from appearing contrived. If ours is a center for Zen spirituality, let's look at the way mountains are drawn in a "Zen fashion"— for that means depicting the Essence.

First of all, we must call to mind that for the Japanese there is a partnership between spiritual and material agencies, and that they see the Law of Heaven as one great motion of eternity.

The second basic tenet has to do with the human being. In Asia, the weakest of all positions is that of the individual who serves only himself. One very old Japanese Zen text tells us, "The man who forgets himself in the service of that which is greater than himself is already immortal. There is nothing you can do to him."

In Asia, much artistic communication is by two media, both intimately related. By writing, we communicate ideas; by painting, we communicate appearance, form, relationships. The brush therefore becomes, in a sense, the instrument of two distinct achievements. One is this formal mind-zero knowledge; the other is the fluid representation of motion, of *Be-ing,* of *Life-ing,* and that is the picture.

In ancient China, the word for writing and picture was the same. Of course in China, as in Egypt, writing began with the pictogram, a figure representing an object. Gradually, however, Chinese writing became a great art for the communication of ideas, the perpetuation of history and record. Painting only slowly became differentiated from it, and in both Japan and China, there is a question as to which is more beautiful, the inscription or the picture. They are often combined because they represent these two levels of communication, first the seeing of the mind, and second the seeing of the Spirit.

In Zen, the principal kind of painting is *sumi,* that is, black and white. The Zen masters did not add color, except perhaps in a few cases where a very pale tonality was used. They did not wish that color should add flesh to the bones of Zen. Sengai is considered the most apt sumi artist in Japan. His Mount Fuji has two lines, or is it only one?

Once when my friend Horisawa San, the Tendai monk of Mount Hiei, gave gifts, he chose a collection of writings of some famous old master. When I asked, "What is the writing about?" Horisawa-san answered, "Oh, that isn't important. The gift is the kanji!"

The Japanese say that black and white is an art of structure; it is an art of the bones; it is an art of essential form. If the great artist is truly a master, he can do it in black and white and you will see the color. If he is not a master, he may have to put all the colors in to prove to you that it is not necessary for you to see the black and white. Is it because he does not know where to put it? Therefore, it is sometimes said that if the artist is absolutely sure, he can do it in black and white. If he is not sure, he will cover his weakness with color. It is the same with many things in life. If we are sure, we can say it in one sentence. If we are not sure, we write a book about it. So often we make things ornate, to cover lack of knowledge, rather than abundance of knowledge.

In sumi art then, we have the same medium as in writing—black in its various gradations. Now, writing or painting is achieved by the bestowing of life upon the brush. One Zen master said that when a great artist is painting, if he took the sword and cut the brush in half, it would bleed just as much as his arm would, because his own blood is in the brush. There is no longer a man with a brush; there is simply a man extending as a brush. This is simply the result of the ability to obliterate or forget the self.

The brush used in Asian art is a circle of bristles usually brought to a point. Its use is determined by a vast number of possible strokes. Many Asians start to use this brush in childhood, because they learn to write with a brush. And gradually they reach a point of proficiency where they are no longer conscious of the brush.

It is like a proficient violinist, who in concert is no longer conscious of the left hand fingering, the right hand bowing, and the memory and emotions totally employed. The artist could not possibly consciously control all these as rapidly as the composition demands. Instantaneous communication of impulse has become "second nature," as we say.

It is the same with the artist and the brush. His fluid coordination of consciousness with the brush enables him to cause it to perform with absolute certainty. There can be no fear, for fear will destroy art, nor can there be doubts or ulterior motives, or break. Just a constant flow that results, say, in a mountain.

Of course the artist starts with a complete internal "visualization." For the Zen artist, the result will be a masterpiece of stark simplicity. It would seem even a child could copy it. But neither the ability to reproduce nor even to trace the mountain is possible.

The mountain, you see, is not on the silk. The silk picture is merely the projection of the artist. It is not a picture by itself, but a mountain brought through the artist's consciousness. Therefore, art of this kind is never literal. So the mountain you see is not a phenomenal mountain.

All the Japanese arts are supposed to be produced from the apex of the artist's consciousness. Theoretically, at least, all of the fine arts and many of the martial arts teach this through meditation. Children are told the artist paints at his best so that the person seeing it may become better. The artist always paints from that which to him is the nearest that he can achieve without distortion to the motion of Heaven itself. This makes the art very important. And can you see why Yamada Roshi, and all the Japanese roshis, feel that a *shiki-shi* (a large card with a hand-written Japanese character) is the most intimate of gifts.

All of us, my friends, are mountains. Whatever we paint, whether we are housewives or bankers or schoolteachers or artists—all of us are continuously projecting an image of ourselves (this koan says a mountain) to the world, to become the environment in which we live. As we grow, our mountain changes. And as we grow in wisdom, our world gradually becomes what it was intended to be, the great teacher, revered, honored, appreciated, and understood—and experienced with a chuckle.

Our mountain is our self-image, projected upon nature, and it looks exactly the way it is forced to look by the kind of projection we ourselves have made. The mountain that we are, we project; and so we create the myriad peaks in the world in which we have to live. But we are *one* mountain among many, the only *one* mountain that is not white.

The qualitative mountain, not of form but of substance, is entirely within ourselves. And whether the mountain means anything is not because *it* is, but rather that *we* are. We are all of us, daily, painting our mountain, and when we have gained a certain level of Zen, our picture reveals it. While Zen is a serious business, we find that it makes us anything but serious. Rather we become a little whimsical, taking great delight in the beauty, joy, and transcendent celebration of our mountain.

Now bring your mountain to dokusan. And I don't want anyone else's mountain!

I leave you the words of Dogen Zenji:

For many years, snow has covered the mountain.
A mountain is washing by the river...
A tiny "hill" is sleeping in its cradle...

SHOGEN'S THREE TURNING WORDS

Why is it that a man of great strength
does not lift up his leg?

It is not with the tongue that we speak.

Why is it that the crimson lines of a clearly
enlightened person never cease to flow?

15

This koan, or part of it, is found as Case 20 of the Mumonkan.

Shogen was a famous Chinese Zen master in the Rinzai tradition. He was a contemporary of Master Mumon, and it's interesting that when Mumon compiled the Mumonkan, he chose some koans of his own era. These particular koans are known as "Turning Words," because they have the power to turn us from delusion to enlightenment.

When Shogen was growing old, and he realized he would have to find a Dharma successor to carry on his work, he made up these three turning words with which to examine his disciples. Great teacher though he was, he didn't have one who could answer, and he died without a successor.

Why is it that a man of great strength does not lift up his leg?
A Japanese Zen master would probably first point to a sumo wrestler as the man of great strength. We are all familiar with their enormous bulk—about three hundred to four hundred pounds of it. Millions of TV screens across the country record how they crouch over their standing line, glare at the opponent eye to eye, and then test first one huge

bulk of leg, crash it to the ground, and then the other. One day in Tokyo, Yamada Roshi and I were watching Wajima, the great *yokozuna* (grand champion) of the time, warming up, lifting those massive appendages; and the Roshi turned to me and said, "Why does the man of great strength not lift up his leg?"

Shibayama Roshi might say to this koan—"Ask the centipede!" And he'd quote the story of a centipede getting so confused intellectually about how it managed all its legs, that it eventually couldn't make them work at all!

"Why?" you ask.

Crack! with the kotsu.

We must throw ourselves away with this "why" and not answer it intellectually. Having recourse to the little you have learned about Zen, you can present an appropriate response. I am certain Shogen had many disciples who could present the koan intellectually. But an ego-conscious intellectual answer is unsatisfactory. And I'm always pleased when I see the apparent dissatisfaction of someone who gives that kind of answer. If there is no ego present, then there are no restrictions. We are free to move our legs or not to move our legs. The real point of the koan is why there is *no-leg* raising?

The next time you see the centipede, look well. It has already cast away its hundred legs, and Mount Mayon walks away happily—quite unaware of its legs. "Why?" Take a look. If you want to know—whether it is pure gold or not, you must look at it in the midst of fire. Burn off the legs! Or take out that two-edged sword and cut them off.

It is not with the tongue that we speak.
This is another easy koan, superficially. It requires no great insight. A vigorous snap of the fingers will bring two or three waiters at a restaurant. We all know that "actions can speak louder than words." But that is not the point of the koan. Nor does it have anything to do with unworthiness or humility. Carefully thought-out answers will only evoke the command, "Say something without moving your lips or tongue!"

Dogen Zenji said, "Abandonment of words and letters is nothing other than every word and phrase."

I can hear the little computers in your mind—which you hope is no-mind—digesting the input. I must transcend words and silence, and when I speak not move the tip of my tongue.

The essence of word is no-word. When speech flows, are we aware of our moving tongue? Or are we aware of its not-moving? This is the point of the koan.

Basho says:

> *With my fan*
> *I mime drinking sake*
> *Falling cherry blossoms.*

A translation by Nobuyuki Yuasa says:

> *Using my fan*
> *For a cup*
> *I pretend to drink*
> *Under the scattering cherry blossoms.*

Aitken Roshi tells us in *Zen Wave:*

> Basho is not pretending; he is miming, and this can be carried a step further. Marcel Marceau is not a mime. He is that kite-flyer, and, sitting there under the falling petals, Basho is actually drinking wine. He is free of bottles, as Marceau is free of string. He is the act itself.
>
> Analytically, we may say that Marceau mimes and that Basho mimes the mime of the Noh actor. So in that sense, Basho is freer than Marceau. He is free of bottles and of the Noh apparatus too—costume, music, stage, audience and the rest.

With empty hands, Marcel Marceau dreams he flies a kite. Basho dreams he is a Noh player, miming, with a fan. "I'm a fire engine! R r r r r r!" shouts the child. We hold our ears and smile patronizingly, imprisoned in our plans for the future and our memories of the past.

Say something without moving your lips or tongue.

R r r r r r!

We celebrate our lives in our koans!

In ending this section, consider this story from an old issue of *TIME* magazine (August 3, 1981):

> [I]n the town of Rockport, Maine, Michael Parents is speaking

of creation. The story Parents tells is from an Iroquois legend, explaining how birds got their song. God, it seems, decided on a fair and just competition. Each bird would fly upward as far as it could, and at that level where its lungs burst and it could fly no higher, it would hear the song it was destined to sing forever. The higher the level, the sweeter and more powerful the song. This was an ingenious idea, even for God, and he was, Mr. Parents points out, "kind of proud of himself, in a Great Spirit sort of way."

Then suddenly, right before everybody's eyes, Parents transforms himself from storyteller into bird. He sinks his neck into his shoulders. He flaps invisible but powerful wings. He crosses his eyes fiercely. His hooked nose curves even more sharply than his downturned mouth. With pride, with paranoia, he twitches his head from side to side. He becomes an eagle, the odds-on favorite to win God's most majestic sound. It may be Sunday morning in Rockport Village in Maine in the year 1981, but now it is also the first day of creation. When Michael Parents' unsuspecting eagle—with a thrush stowed away on its back, lifts off majestically at the upward wave of the storyteller's hand, the audience lifts too, out the window of the room, above the sun-dappled boats lying at anchor in Rockport Harbor, beyond time, beyond space. Somewhere off in a primeval woods, everybody's inner ear hears a sneaky, undeserving little hitchhiker of a thrush, trill the loveliest of songs.

Why is it that the crimson lines of a clearly enlightened person never cease to flow?
Yamada Roshi, in his Mumonkan, translates this koan as, "Why is it that a man of the enlightened eye does not cut off the crimson purple line?" Yamada Roshi's interpretation goes beyond transcending the "why." The man of satori that he is, he asks the question very simply, "Why are properly accomplished saints and bodhisattvas attached to the red-purple line, the line of tears?" And he answers just as simply, "Because they are tears of mercy and compassion."

Why are perfectly accomplished saints and bodhisattvas attached to their zafus? Because the zafu is the source of mercy and compassion.

From the point of view of Zen, the formation of the human personality is the polishing away of dualistic thinking, which is the removal of one's delusions, so that one's original nature comes to the fore. If we look up to somebody as a "great and admirable person" it is not because that person has amassed a great amount of money, or has some high position in government or whatever—but because we see that person as having taken unto himself the sufferings of others. In other words, that person has done away with all dualistic opposition between himself and others. If "the other" sheds tears of sorrow, that person sheds tears too. If joy, joy is reciprocated. Enlightenment brings deep inner peace, even in the face of death.

I recall the Zen story of a woman in a state of utter sorrow, with plenty of tears flowing, but still maintaining a sense of serenity and peacefulness, through it all. She was a disciple of Hakuin Zenji (during the Edo period in Japan) and was called "festive lady" for her jovial character. This person attained a deep state of enlightenment, and had a very clear enlightened eye. She married and had children, who in turn also married and had children of their own. One of these children was especially dear to the now elderly lady. When the child died suddenly, the old lady wept and wept in her sorrow. Someone seeing this asked her how, being deeply enlightened, she could cry so much. In reply, the old lady said that her every tear is a pearl that shines in full brightness.

Father Hendricks, a scripture scholar in Manila, paraphrases the fourth Beatitude, "Blessed are those who identify with those who need mercy." No separation at all, the call of the maya bird urges us home—and the call is mutually enriching. There is an old pious saying in the Church, "When God calls someone, He makes them what He calls them."

Why are perfectly accomplished saints and bodhisattvas attached to the crimson line? We see right here in our zendo, not quite yet perfectly accomplished saints and bodhisattvas attached to the tears of mercy and compassion.

This part of the koan has to do with the "after sitting" Zen! The other day, I came across some notes I made during a Japanese teisho the Roshi gave on the Hekiganroku, when I was in Japan. Listen. He is telling us to get our Zen into action:

> It is regrettable if your Zen is in your eye only—then it becomes a shadow. Kensho painted in the head (remembered) is false. The better you *know,* the calmer you become—you lose yourself and become kinder, and become as your True

Self is. If it is not so, you have yourself, the false self and aggressive ego and you are disillusioned—and you're holding horse manure in your hands.

I beg each of you to see what you're holding in your hands each day this week.

ORYU'S THREE TURNING WORDS

How is my hand like the Buddha's hand?

How is my leg like a donkey's leg?

All people have their own place of birth in karma.
Where is your place of birth in karma?

16

In the year 1230, at Zuigan Temple in China's Mei State, Master
Mumon, whose famous book The Gateless Gate *(Mumonkan)* we use
in koan study, was invited to give a series of teisho on the forty cases
that make up his book. This he did. His host was Master Muryo Soju,
who expressed his gratitude to Mumon by writing a short verse to each
of the parts of the above koan. Oryu, the Zen master who checked his
disciples with these koans, was famous in the Rinzai line, and had been
dead about two hundred years at the time Muryo wrote the poems.
These koans, with the poems, are as follows:

> How is my hand like the Buddha's hand?
> *Groping for the pillow at my back, I could feel it.*
> *In spite of myself, I burst out laughing.*
> *From the first, the whole body is the hand.*
>
> How is my leg like a donkey's leg?
> *Even before taking a step, I have already trodden the ground.*
> *Freely I pass over the four seas just as I wish.*
> *I ride topsy-turvy on Yogi's three-legged donkey.*

All people have their own place of birth in karma.
Everything penetrates to the world prior to consciousness.
Nada broke his bones and gave them back to his father.
Did the fifth Patriarch have to rely on a causal relation with a father?

Let's look at each pair in turn.

How is my hand like the Buddha's hand?

For over thirty years, Master Oryu would examine his disciples by holding out his hand and saying, "Why is my hand like Buddha's hand?" We know it is fundamental in Zen to cast away the self. When there is no self, there is no discrimination, such as my hand and Buddha's hand. Is Oryu then saying there is no difference between my hand and Buddha's hand? I am a person very conscious of hands and I always notice them. No two people have the same hands. Hands are very distinctive. And how would Oryu know what Buddha's hand looked like anyway?

Many times over the years, I have been with Yamada Roshi and have heard him refer to his own two hands. He says, "Everyone has two hands. When we are absorbed in doing something with both hands, we are not aware of them. My two hands are in fact living my life, which is not two. From life's point of view, there are not two hands."

Behold the Kannon of mercy with a thousand hands!

Shibayama Roshi has said, "When you see, all of yourself is the eye. So it is not called seeing any longer. When you hear, all of yourself is the ear. So it is not called hearing any longer. When you walk, all of yourself is the foot, so it is not called walking any longer. If you do not grasp this secret in your own experience, you are a stranger to Zen, no matter how beautifully you may talk about it."

When you use your hand, all of yourself is the hand!

Waking in the middle of the night, Muryo reached up for the pillow and felt IT.

Ho! Ho! He burst out laughing. The hand, his hand, and Buddha's hand and the whole body and all the universe was there! *Ho! Ho! Ho!*

This verse is Muryo's kensho-ki. It's in very short form, very concise and all there.

Gutei lifts a finger, Shakyamuni twirls a flower, Nansen kills a cat, Kyozan strikes the stand with a gavel, Ryutan blows out the candle,

Tony washes his feet, and Muryo gropes for a pillow. Indeed everything goes back to the same root.

Perhaps I have said too much. When we speak to others we are supposed to say only three-quarters of it. Like Mumon, I have poured out my intestines and belly! But it is still only knowledge. *Knowledge (Prajna)* can never be transmitted. In the final analysis, kensho is your business, with, as Dogen states, "some help from beyond."

How is my leg like a donkey's leg?

The second of Master Oryu's three barriers has to do with legs. Showing his leg to his disciples, he used to question them, "Why is my leg like a donkey's leg?"

Show me!

Now the beautiful verse that Muryo appended:

> *Even before taking a step, I have already arrived.*
> *Freely I pass over the four seas just as I wish.*
> *I ride backward on Yogi's three-legged donkey.*

Even before taking a step, I have already arrived. Your destination is no other place, but where you are now. How can any place in the universe not be home?

Consider Psalm 139:

> *Where could I go to escape your spirit?*
> *Where could I flee from your presence?*
> *If I climb to the heavens, you are there,*
> *There too, if I lie in Sheol.*
> *If I flew to the point of sunrise*
> *Or westward across the sea...*

In the poem, Muryo calls this sea, the four seas. And a Zen person can freely fly to this point, and so the poem says "Freely I pass over the four seas, just as I wish." But this does not refute Meister Eckhart's statement, "The more you seek God, the less you will find God."

The last line, "I ride backward on Yogi's three-legged donkey," refers to an old koan:

> Once a monk asked Master Yogi, "What is Buddha?"

"A three-legged donkey goes by clattering his hoofs," replied Master Yogi.

So this time our Essential Nature is under the guise of a three-legged donkey. In another koan we see *IT* as Keichu's Carts (Mumonkan, Case 8). All koans deal with our Essential Nature, and we must not be confused by outward appearances, nor by the information that you are to ride *backward* on a three-legged donkey. Once you are deeply into your practice, you can do this very easily. Getting into your practice deeply is the whole business of sesshin. Silence is of absolute necessity for sesshin, and we are finding it is increasingly difficult to locate a venue that will support our silence.

But to get back to the original question, "How is my leg like a donkey's leg?" Cases 58 and 59 in the Hekiganroku say, "The supreme Way is not difficult, it merely avoids picking and choosing." If the supreme Way does not choose, what are we doing with all this duality, my leg and a donkey's leg! There's a pit-hole here. Don't fall into it.

But still, show me: How is my leg like a donkey's leg!

All people have their own place of birth in karma.
When an ordinary person is asked, "Where were you born?" they answer without hesitation. But a Zen disciple who has at least the intellectual knowledge of the Essential World, treats this question as a Dharma combat—and will sit there with eyes glaring, wondering what to answer.

Shakyamuni taught his monks, "There is an unborn, an unoriginated, an unmade, an uncompounded. Were there not, oh mendicants, there would be no escape from the world of the born, the originated, the made, and the compounded."

Everyone has her own place of birth in the karma, says Oryu. Is he presenting us a dichotomy? No duality here. The Essential World and the phenomenal world have been one ever since the beginning—whenever that was! Don't fall into a hole that isn't there. Don't gouge healthy flesh.

Our physical body is given by our parents—and is temporal and subject to coming and going. When we have transcended this we plunge directly into "What is your Primal Face before your parents are born?" As Shibayama Roshi says, it invites you to be born anew to the eternal True Self. The True Self is your parents' Primal Face before your grandparents are born. And is and was and will be all tumbled around together. The past is gone. The future will never come.

You know, one person new to koans once told me, "Do you mind if I don't read your teisho on the koan until after I have completed the dokusan? Your teisho confuse me." This is the supreme compliment. Teisho are *meant* to confuse!

When I said previously I sometimes say too much, I was referring to the field of intellectual understanding. I don't have to tell you that there is an intellectual understanding to the koans. Eventually you can explain every part of them—this means this and that means that—and you have killed the koan. It has lost its life. A good teisho will wander around, not make much sense, take any number of detours to keep the intellect from jumping to the "logical conclusion." It's the job of the teisho to keep the intellect from leaping, and prod *it* to leap forth.

A long period of sitting prior to dokusan is of enormous importance. You hear me ask koan people for three hours of sitting between dokusans. We need time in the desert before the combat. A sesshin provides a good ambience, and should be a real desert experience.

Sesshin is the desert and has its own special time. Something should happen at sesshin that does not happen any other time. In the sesshin desert, you can perhaps reach a deep state of consciousness—and you put a koan before that deep state, and the koan lives and moves and has its being as it melts, blocks, and sets freedom free. A sesshin should be full of *Ho! Ho! Ho!'s.*

Buddha's hand, donkey's leg, and the cause of birth. They are neither Buddha, nor Tao, nor Zen.

Buddha's hand is the mind of everyman—the hand of God, the beggar, the swindler, the spouse, the boss, the maid, the prisoner, and the president. How does my hand compare with the Buddha's hand?

The donkey's leg will take us on all life's journeys—into joy, into surprise, into the desert, into despair, into failure, into hope, into the hearts of others. And we will find ourselves where we have been all the time, right here.

Everybody has a place of birth in karma. And Meister Eckhart too has something to say about it:

> And *"in this birth*
> *you will discover*
> *all blessing."*

Neglect this birth
and you neglect
all blessing.
Tend only to this birth in you
and you will find there
all goodness and all consolation
all delight
all being and all truth.

TOSOTSU'S THREE BARRIERS

The purpose of making one's way through grasses
And asking a Master about the subtle truth
Is only to realize one's self-nature.
Now you venerable monks,
Where is your self-nature at this very moment?

When you have attained your self-nature,
You can free yourself from life and death.
How would you free yourself from life and death
When the light of your eyes is falling to the ground
[when you are about to die]?

When you have freed yourself from life and death,
You know where to go.
After your four elements have decomposed
Where will you go?

17

Let's examine each piece in turn.

The purpose of making one's way through grasses and asking a Master about the subtle truth is only to realize one's self-nature. Now you venerable monks, where is your self-nature at this very moment?
The first part of this koan sounds like a trip to a quiet resort to do sesshin, doesn't it? It's nice and cool there, and there is so much green around.

It reminds me of a poem said to be written by Dantika, a Buddhist nun and contemporary of Shakyamuni:

As I left my daytime resting place on Vulture Peak
I saw an elephant
Come up on to a riverbank
After its bath.
A man took a hook,
and said to the elephant,
"Give me your foot."
The elephant stretched out its foot;
the man mounted.
Seeing that which was wild before
gone tame under human hands
I went into the forest
And concentrated my mind.

How appropriate! "I went into the forest and concentrated my mind." Or, as we might say, "I went to Scarboro for sesshin."

In Zen, grasses and underbrush mean delusions. In Zen, delusions are the opposite of reality. For example, I'm here now—but what you see and hear and touch and smell is as much a delusion as putting a photo on the altar is a delusion. That is why we say a picture of food never fills a hungry stomach. We must sweep away the delusions—all the pictures. Zen is an emptying process that will bring us to Reality. I'd like to point out that this emptying is not making a hole to be filled with desirable things. This emptying is getting down to something that is already there—something submerged in baggage and garbage, something indescribable, of great beauty, and inexhaustible richness.

St. Paul tells us we do not have to find that unity, we already possess it. Our task he says, is to *preserve* it. That for which you are searching in sitting, you already possess. Yamada Roshi used to tell us often that we already have everything we need and want.

Another way of putting this emptying process is "to get rid of the self." As we say in the Beatitudes, "Blessed are those who lose their lower selves, they shall find their true selves." Master Shido Bunan says, "Die while alive, and be completely dead—then do whatever you will; all is good." (Shades of Augustine—"Love God and do what you will.")

Coming to see that all is good is coming to see with the third eye—coming to "see" our self-nature. This has to happen by direct experience. Yamada Roshi always uses the verb *tsukamaeru*—"to grasp." To grasp the Empty-Infinite. The self-nature. Those are very strong words indeed!

But we need strong words here, because this is *the* Fundamental. And I'd like to add something personal here. Living *this* is what I call faith. For many years, I had a problem with that word. The old catechism used to define faith as the intellectual assent to divinely revealed truths. Once I became steeped in Zen, I found that definition experientially inadequate. And then one day, I came across a definition of faith that "fit" for me—just like a well-fitting lid on a box.

Strangely enough, the book was not from Asia, but rather from Africa. There is an institute in Kenya parallel to the Jesuit-run East Asian Pastoral Institute in Quezon City, Manila, and one of their publications defines the life of faith as trying to respond to God's presence (I like to say "God's Be-ing") in our life at all times and places. This of course presupposes a Divine Being. (Divine *Be*-ing.) Zen says we must grasp "This," the Empty-Infinite, God, experientially. We have a lot we can do to prepare ourselves for the experience, but in the end IT is finally a vivifying gift, which aspect of life we call love.

Zen leads us along the Way to experience that Supreme Being, characterized as Wisdom and Compassion. Once faith springs to action, we have spirituality. A mystic would say spirituality is allowing the Supreme Being to return to its original spontaneity in our life. Paul put it in a nutshell—"I live, not I, but Christ lives within me."

In the meantime, we heed the advice found in the verse of Mumonkan Case 33, which gives us a hint of appropriate action:

> *If you meet a swordsman, you may present a sword.*
> *You should not offer a poem unless you meet a poet.*
> *When you speak to others, say only three-quarters of it.*
> *You should never give the remaining part.*

By the way, where is the self-nature right now—at this very moment. As Shibayama Roshi says, "Unless you are established in your own definite experience, you can never answer this question. If you say yes, such relativistic affirmation has to go. If you say no, such dead negation has to be smashed away. You must 'let go your hold on the edge of the precipice.'"

Where is the self-nature right now? Quick! Show me!

When you have attained your self-nature, you can free yourself from life and death. How would you free yourself from life and death when the light of your eyes is falling to the ground [when you are about to die]?
Shibayama Roshi says, "If you realize your own nature, you certainly are free from life and death."

Life and death are superficial changes in the phenomenal world, Zen tells us. This is staggering when we first become aware of it. In the Essential World there is nothing to be called "life" and "death." They are useless distinctions, according to the old Zen masters. One of the old patriarchs used to say, "Within me there is neither life nor death." What a paradox for all of us.

Some of you may know that Nanzenji, the famous Rinzai Temple in Kyoto, was very important to me during my early Zen training. Its founder, Master Daimin, wrote the following poem on his deathbed:

> *In coming I have no abode*
> *In leaving I have no fixed direction.*
> *How is it ultimately?*
> *Here I am all the time.*

That is the living of what I have often said—Zen is not doing anything, it is not going anywhere, it is simply being, *experiencing* fully all the time, yesterday, today, and tomorrow. "Here I am all the time!" This should be true for us every moment of our lives.

We hear this too in the Bible: "Where are you, Samuel?" "Here I am, Lord!"

Here I am all the time. In his teisho, Yamada Roshi asks, "When you are at the very point of death, how will you free yourself from the horror and agony of death?"

Ryutan, the fine Zen master who lit a lantern for Tokusan so that he could see his way home in the dark, handed it to Tokusan and then blew it out! In so doing he blew out the darkness for Tokusan to come to enlightenment at that moment. When Ryutan was dying, it is said he cried out and struggled in agony. He said to his amazed disciples surrounding him, "I tell you, my agonized crying is not different at all from my joyful singing."

Perhaps the best of all Zen sayings about dying is the story of Master Bankai.

> Master Bankai was visited by an old man who begged, "My last hour is approaching; please teach me how to prepare myself for death."
> "No preparation is needed," answered Master Bankai.
> "Why is it unnecessary?" asked the old man.
> "When the time comes for you to die, just die," said Bankai.

Death! The great barrier for all of us. I ask you the question again, "When you are at the very point of death, how will you free yourself from the horror and agony of death?"

When you have freed yourself from life and death, you know where to go. After your four elements have decomposed, where will you go? Ancient Indian thought held that all matter consists of the four elements of earth, water, fire, and wind; and that after death the physical body decomposes into these original elements.

In any case, this barrier is addressed not only to Zen disciples but to all. And human beings have feelings and emotions about this barrier, which we must pass. Master Tosotsu, out of compassion, tries to eradicate such emotional attachments as ours.

I think Saint John was trying to do the same thing when he said in his first letter (1 John 3:1–3):

> My dear people, we are already the children of God, but what we are to be in the future, has not yet been revealed: all we know, is that when it is revealed, we shall be like him, because we shall see him as he really is.

To paraphrase Dogen Zenji, "life and death, as it is, Essential life." At one instant "this," at another instant "that"—all are not apart from me. As Shibayama Roshi said, "How can there be anything that is not the newly born True Self?" Listen to Master Ryokan's death poem:

> *Showing now its front side.*
> *Now its back,*

Falls the maple leaf.

Where is the maple leaf?

As I said at the beginning, this is a koan about the Great Matter—and it affects us all because one day we must all pass through that ultimate barrier.

Zen would have us not be solemn. When Tosotsu himself was dying, he gathered his disciples around his bed, showed them his last poem, and died serenely.

> *Forty-eight years—*
> *I am all done with the ignorant and the wise.*
> *I am not a hero.*
> *My way to Nirvana is serene and peaceful.*

Serene and peaceful.
Here I am all the time.
Here I am—right here—right now.
When you have died, you will know where to go.
So? Where do you go?
Right here. Right now. Quickly!

KIDO'S THREE BARRIERS

How is it that someone whose eyes are not opened
puts on clothes and skirts made of empty sky?

How is it that someone who surveys land and digs wells
cannot evade that?

How is it that someone who plunges into the sea and counts
all the sands is sitting on top of a needle?

18

The three koans seem to be quite different and separate, and yet for me they all go back to the same root: *Tathagata*—just that.
    Master Sogyo has a poem:

> *Taking along Shakyamuni Tathagata, Manjusri, and Momyo*
> *I enjoy the mountain spring*
> *visiting one truth after another.*

Manjusri is the bodhisattva of wisdom, the highest; and Momyo is the lowest bodhisattva, the bodhisattva of beginners. They tag along with Shakyamuni, all just as they are, as they savor the mountain spring—and visit one truth after another! Each as it is! Oh that we could do that!

How is it that someone whose eyes are not opened
puts on clothes and skirts made of empty sky?
How is it that one who is not enlightened can put on clothes and skirts

made of emptiness? Clothes and skirts—it seems to me that here we have the world of phenomena—*shiki*—form and color. When we "take" clothes and skirts as they are, what do we have? Well, the koan suggests that we have emptiness. And this is just what the Heart Sutra says: "Form is nothing but emptiness. Emptiness is nothing but form." Perhaps this would be an appropriate place to read a verse I received from one of the sitters at Bago Bantay, in the Philippines, a political detainee who saw a piece of old dried-up grass that was made of emptiness:

from counting breath, one to ten
makyo and tense body
and ache of dedication
and love of zazen
opening myself and closing
cause and effect are one
what is essential is the way
with thought that is no-thought
i see form that is no-form
the driest blade of grass
probing mu to my very essence
stopping the sound
of a distant temple bell
moving mountains
i draw water from a well
that has not been dug
from counting breath
to the driest blade of grass
there is no difference
there are no images
there is no gap

I'd like to review with you Yamada Roshi's teaching about "emptiness." As I repeatedly tell you, in this Essential World the logic of the absolute reigns. This means one thing is the whole; the whole is one thing. When you realize this Essential World, you will understand that you and the whole universe are one.

When you stick up one finger, there is nothing but the finger in the whole universe. Just the finger—the finger and the whole universe are one. This is seeing in the absolute. This can be true, because the finger, having no substance, is empty. This emptiness is nothing but the essential nature of the finger. The substance of all things is emptiness. The subject is empty; the object is empty. And the subject and object are one in emptiness from the very beginning. The ordinary common sense subject and object oppose each other. There is you, seeing with your eyes, and there is an external object seen by you. This is true not only for sight, but for all our senses. For the truly enlightened eye, however, this dualistic contrast is nothing but illusion produced by one's bifurcating intellect.

But even emptiness is a concept, and can only be emptied as a concept when it is cancelled by its opposite! Because in Zen, when all opposites find their convergence in experience, they cancel each other out. Therefore, it represents that *experience,* and we have to refer to the Empty-Infinite, or the emptiness that is full!

In the Hannya Shingyo we recite: "All phenomena are nothing but emptiness; emptiness is nothing but all phenomena." So clothes and skirts are nothing but emptiness. How can an unenlightened person put on empty clothes?

How is it that someone who surveys land and digs wells cannot evade *that*?

In ancient times, surveyors were regarded as particularly intelligent people. For our era, we might perhaps change the question to "Why is it that an intelligent person who can master advanced physics cannot surpass *that*?" "Or why is it that Juanito, who can make excellent mayonnaise, cannot surpass *that*."

Obviously, here we have a koan that's a bit different. It is very seldom indeed that we speak of intellect in a koan, but here it is, an intelligent person. Intelligence suggests quality. We use the word, and that which it points to, as a compliment. We talk about the *quality* of our sitting. Anyone can make an effort to cross the legs and sit—but I'm talking about *really* silencing the body to harmony, really silencing the mind to harmony. We speak of the quality of our presence. We are physically and geographically located somewhere at all times, but what is the *quality* of our presence.

We are not about to ask you if your life is going anywhere. Something like that would be the antithesis of Zen. Zen simply tells us that we have only to deal with the here and now. With the dynamism of our

Essential Nature empowering our intelligence, how do we deal with the here and now? With the dynamism of our Essential Nature returned to its original spontaneity by the assiduous practice of sitting and awareness of being openness to the Ultimate Reality—does it make any difference what we do?

When our alarm clock goes off in the morning, and we stretch and rub our eyes, can we possibly do anything to surpass that? And then when we swing our legs over the side of the bed and put our feet on the floor, can anything surpass that? And when we go over to the sink and splash water on our face, can anything surpass that?

When your child comes running with a cut finger, you put on a Band-Aid. When an old man has been knocked down by a car in front of your house, you rush him to the hospital. No great heroics—you just *do* it! If your house is untidy, you clean it up.

Fidelity to this way of living is commitment or dedication—and I suggest that gradually the pain will ease. Probably we will never be sufficiently empty that all our spontaneous actions are 100 percent appropriate, but we do our best, peacefully, and it can be said of us, "They are without guile." Truly *that* cannot be surpassed.

How is it that someone who plunges into the sea and counts all the sands is sitting on top of a needle?
In ancient China, there was a saying that a wise man can count all the sands in the sea. There is a Filipino saying: "A wise person can count all the hairs on the back of a cat." How about Canada? What innumerability can a wise Canadian count? (There's probably a witty political response to that!)

Somone who plunges into the sea and counts all the sands is surely a person of supra-normal powers. Perhaps a disembodied spirit could do it, but then the next part of the koan refutes this. It asks how it is that he is sitting on top of a needle. To sit on top of a needle is to occupy space.

I think you are familiar with enough koans to know that the first thing to do is identify this "someone." If both subject and object are empty, who is this someone? Whoever the someone is, his *thusness* is nothing else than himself: for instance, a man living here in Toronto in 2007, seeking reconciliation and peace.

There was an Old Testament sage who said that peace comes from integrity. In relation to this, I want to share an experience I had in

Cubao, in the Philippines. One Saturday morning, I was entertained for two hours in front of a store that puts on a live Christmas play on the broad ledge along the second floor of the building facing the street. At that time, the theme was the traditional one: there was Bethlehem and the hills and sheep and Joseph came along, a wooden life-size figurine manipulated electronically, leading a donkey carrying Mary, and they entered the cave (somewhat uncertainly, because this was the first try-out for the producers, and the many mishaps and near misses provided abundant humor!). Joseph came out of the cave and went to the nearby mountain and gathered some hay, and trotted back to the cave and tried to let the hay fall in the crib. To the enjoyment of the onlookers, it fell everywhere but the place it was suppose to fall. After about ten tries, success was achieved. There was nothing wrong with the electricity. It was always working. But the movable parts of the wooden figurine were not coordinated at first, to allow the electricity to work properly. Eventually, the handicap was overcome, and a quality akin to "integrity" took over.

In our *bashar* (body) and *nephesh* (mind), we are like wooden figurines, given life by the electricity of our Essential Nature. Without coordination, there is no integrity. Lack of coordination may come from a malfunctioning body or mind, which is sickness and requires medical attention. Or it comes from delusions, which abound in our lives, and which act as blocks or idols.

To be our own true Tathagata, we have to get rid of delusion. There are two means for this: sitting, and, as the Buddhists say, allowing our Essential Nature to return to its own spontaneity. Faithful practice will gradually bring you peace. If you feel this is slow in coming to fruition, then perhaps you are not sitting enough, or perhaps the quality of your sitting leaves something to be desired. When this has been adjusted, I promise you that integrity will come with peace in its wake, and you will bring to your own life, to your family life, to your business world, and to your waiting country, a quality of presence that is totally wise— and all the while, sitting on top of a needle.

JOSHU'S THREE TURNING WORDS

The Buddha made of wood will not pass through fire;
if he does, he will surely be burnt.

The Buddha made of clay will not pass through water;
if he does, he will surely drown.

The Buddha made of metal will not pass through a
furnace; if he does, he will surely melt.

Joshu says, "The true Buddha is sitting in the recesses
of the house."

19

As Aitken Roshi says in his teisho on Mu, "Joshu was a remarkable teacher in a remarkable era." His dates are 778–897, so he is said to have lived almost a hundred and twenty years! He lived during the T'ang dynasty, the golden age of Zen in China. Zen teachers are noted for their longevity and many lived into their eighties and nineties. This is not so remarkable today, but it was then. Let us see if his life reveals his secret.

Joshu was ordained a priest as a young boy, and at eighteen years of age went to study Zen with Nansen. At the time of their first meeting, Nansen was sick in bed. He asked the young seeker the leading question a master usually asks to discern if the new disciple knows of any other world except the materialistic phenomenal world. In Zen that question can be: "Where have you come from?"

Joshu replied, "From the place of the Auspicious Image." This is a famous statue of the dying Shakyamuni in a reclining position. Nansen asked, "Did you see the Auspicious Image?" Joshu replied, "I did not see the image, but I have seen a reclining Tathagata." Nansen recognized the promise of the young man and accepted him as a disciple. Joshu stayed with Nansen for forty years.

After Nansen's death, Joshu set out on a pilgrimage to visit outstanding Zen masters so that he could deepen and clarify his realization. The announcement he made before starting is often quoted, and considering the Confucian veneration of elders and pampering of children, it is a remarkable resolution. He said, "If I meet a seven-year-old child who can teach me, I will become that child's student. If I meet a hundred-year-old man who seeks my guidance, I will be his teacher."

Finally, at the age of eighty, he settled at a place called Joshu (from which he got his name), and accepted disciples. His gentle teaching is called "lips and mouth Zen" and his disciples claimed to be able to see a soft golden light playing around his lips as he spoke. Yamada Roshi often says, "Joshu's Zen was quiet Zen." You might point out that at the age of one hundred and over there's not much energy left to be anything but quiet. Be that as it may, Joshu was a great Zen teacher.

Many of the famous masters frequently used what is called "turning words" in their teaching. These are the words that master used to "turn" their disciples from illusion to insight, from darkness to enlightenment. The turning words that Joshu used are the ones at the top of this chapter.

There was an incident in the Manila zendo that gave all of us, but especially Yamada Roshi, much delight. At one time there was in the zendo a beautiful Buddha made of wood. When I left Japan, some of my Japanese friends gave me, as a farewell gift, a trip to India and Nepal. In the souvenir shops in Kathmandu, I found myself confronted with hundreds of inexpensive statues of the Buddha. The favorite there depicts Shakyamuni coming out of his *satori,* extending his right hand to touch the ground, signifying his wish to return to the world of men.

There were literally hundreds of statues there, which at first glance looked all the same. But upon more careful inspection, I noticed there were little subtle differences, and in the end it took me quite a while to choose the one I liked best.

One person, Sakina, loved the statue and, although we kept it in storage most of the time, at every available chance she put it out. "I'm like Joshu's dog after Buddha," she used to say. One day, when she met me at the airport as I returned from Leyte, she had a half-tragic, half-comic look on her face. She greeted me quickly and then blurted out, "The dog got Buddha!" I first thought she must have had kensho, but she went on to explain that one of the convent dogs got into our cushion room and ate the Buddha up—but not completely! For Sakina it was a case of Joshu's dog getting even!

When I examined the statue I saw that it had been irreparably damaged, so I wrapped it carefully in newspaper and put a match to it. A Buddha made of wood won't pass through fire; if he does, he'll surely be burned.

A corollary to this was told by another young woman, also in Manila. It seems when she graduated from university she joined a "subversive" group. When she complained of its godlessness, she was sent to see a priest also in the movement. He brought a crucifix. He set fire to it and they both stood and watched it burn to ashes. "There!" he said, "God is all gone." The god made of wood won't pass through fire; if he does, he'll be all gone.

One Christmas Eve, at 6 P.M., about fifty armed men surrounded one of our barrios in Leyte. Some of these men entered the house of the barrio captain, handcuffed her and her family and led them away to the meeting place for a dialogue with the barrio people. The husband was taken away separately out of sight, and three shots were soon heard from that direction. One of the people of the barrio asked permission to speak. "Sir, why did you take that man away? He is a good man. No one in this barrio wants to have him killed. God doesn't want us Filipinos to kill one another." The leader thrust out his weapon and shouted, "This gun is our god!"

The god or Buddha made of metal will surely pass away, too.

And then the leader continued with words that we usually place on the lips of kings and those who live in palaces and high places: "And Amahan, Anak, and Espiritu Santo are *pamahaw, pani-udto,* and *pani-hapon!*" (Father, Son and Holy Spirit are our breakfast, lunch, and supper.)

A lot of us make a god of our stomach. Surely that too will pass away.

And there is the Biblical passage that always comes to mind when I hear this koan:

> As he was leaving the Temple, one of his disciples said to him,
> "Look teacher, what wonderful stones and what wonderful

buildings!" And Jesus said to him, "You see these great buildings? Not a single stone will be left on another; everything will be destroyed." (Mark 13:1)

The god or buddha made of stone will surely pass away too.
And what about the god or buddha made of gold?
The god or buddha made of gold…and the god or buddha of beauty! (How tempting!)

I'm certain it is eminently clear by now that all these images of Buddha made of wood and clay and metal are our idols. Paul tells us we all have our idols, that we are all secret worshippers. Maybe our idol is not an image of Shakyamuni (and do you understand now why Joshu told Nansen that he did *not* see the Auspicious Image—the idol—but rather he "saw" Something Else?) Let us be humble enough to admit that we have our idols. Even if it is not someone or something else, it is most certainly the idol of ourselves, which is called our ego. That is the false images we should be working to eliminate…so that it too will pass away.

After all, what is an image? It is a representation of someone or something. It is not the real thing. It is static, and the real person is alive! I think of the well-known story of a new widow who was studying photographs of her late husband and then cast them down and cried out in despair, "I cannot even remember what he looked like!" Of course she couldn't. Every day of their life together, she lived with a living person whose facial expressions were always changing and relevant to the moment. People in life are in constant flux and change. Although many of us as we grow old may wish it were so, we just can't go on giving the same face to others every day or every year.

Every day we're a different person. Every day is indeed a new day. Every meeting is a fresh start. In order to give that fresh start a chance, Zen tells us that we have to have space for it. We have to give it room to operate. Hence the necessity of *emptying*. That is why Ruben Habito, when he is asked what Zen is for him, always replies, "Zen is emptying!"

The last of Joshu's words is, "The true Buddha is sitting in the recesses of the house." How simple—to sit in the house. Our complicated lives today are dependent on factors and elements and conditions *outside* of ourselves, outside the house. Zen is an experience of internal security. Outside the house, we tend to mistake complexity for intelligence.

We have come to fear the simple as something primitive and inadequate, and tend to worship the tremendous mass of knowledge loose in the world today. Our memory bank becomes complicated and full of tensions and problems. Right here I'd like to enumerate what we can do.

1. Simplify our life. There are wide impications here. Environmentalists are pleding with us to simlify our lives to save the planet.

2. Simplify of our attitudes. At the early stages, we can to a certain degree, weaken them by rationalization. Deep feelings can also be lessened if they are articulated.

3. Endeavor to "let go" consciously. If we don't let go of our garbage, it will pollute us. If we find this difficult, we can at least ignore our disqueting impulses. An egoist cannot stand to be ignored.

I tend to hold Western psychology at arm's length. One of the reasons for this is its reliance on memory sequences in psychotherapy. In Zen, we can hardly conceive of an individual recounting a long and difficult life in order to untangle it. Although many of us know, through experience, that roubled people can regain compusre by articulating what is bothering them (if they can name it). In any case, help seems to be available, in a broad sense, by simplifying one's life.

Kensho is a kind of absolute simplification. The immediate experience is in an instant and factual, so it can release the individual from many years of addiction to negative and habitual mental complexities. To support this, Zen has developed a series of remarkable disciplines. We start by relaxing away from a problem rather than by overcoming it by force—a kind of self-discipline that often leads to neurosis. Zen says we have a basic harmonious, gracious, kindly, creative, friendly, and whimsical relationship with life anyway. So in times of tension, turn to that. It can be done, although the first few times will take some effort. So our lives become a series of small victories of insight over ignorance. Sitting in the house will gradually take the urgency out of memory, and then we can learn both how to remember and how to forget. They are curiously interrelated. Blocking bad habits may end in paranoia. You know we can simply allow them to die from lack of nutrition.

The Buddhas sitting in the house, in their gentle, quiet, and slightly humorous Zen way, discover things of importance without their seeming too important; let go of things that are unimportant. Temperament, they say, improves as appreciation of values improves. If the person supported by daily sitting just quietly moves in and accomplishes the adjustments, they gradually become simpler. Much of the delay we experience is argument and analysis. Once we inwardly resolve to change, we can change. At least we turn a corner. If that corner-turning is the time of kensho, we have added impetus. Then, through continuous regular sitting and garbage disposal, gentle growing, kindly relationships, and a devout determination (Bob Aitken calls it "willing") to keep faith with the Zen way (which we can call by the beautiful name of *Life*), gradually we will be made new.

"The true Buddha is sitting in the house," is *Life*. It strikes me that in that koan the verb *sitting* is an active verb en route, so to speak. In the first part of the koan we had passive verbs, "is made of" in connection with the Buddha. Here now is *Life*. The one root that everything goes back to is the *ruach*—breath (*ruach* is Hebrew for the breath of God).

Martin Buber, the great German Jewish theologian, says the point of conversion, transformation in his life, came when he was eleven years old. One evening, after supper on the farm, he wandered out to the barn to see his favorite horse. He stepped on a stool to pat the horse's mane, and all of a sudden as he was patting the horse, he experienced the *Life* that was in the animal connecting with the *Life* in him and the *Life* in the stool and the *Life* in all the universe! For that brief moment, there was only that dynamic field—the very antithesis of any static image!

Read the kensho accounts of people who have had that experience; read the writings of the Zen people through hundreds of years! Father Arevalo, as he officially opened our zendo in the Philippines, said: "Every particle of creation is filled with God!" I used to define Zen spirituality as "responding appropriately to God's presence in each situation we meet," but perhaps that is too egotistical.

Zen is letting the *Life* within us really "live" us! Yamada Roshi says there is no greater service we can do on this earth than diminish the ego by sitting so that the Infinite Life within us can "take over." Saint Paul says, "So that I can say, I live now not I, but Christ lives within me." Even that is perhaps a little intellectual. I prefer the mystics' succinct, "So that Christ in us can say 'Abba' to his Father."

And this too is why Meister Eckhart can say, "God is not found in the soul by adding anything, but by a process of abstraction." And, "God does not ask anything else of you except that you let yourself go and let God be God in you."

Allow things to happen, and find out every day that Zen is an experience of internal security. And so the true God, the true Buddha, is not made of wood or clay or metal or flesh or bone; is not tall or short or fat or thin; has not black skin or white skin or brown skin or yellow skin; is not Jew or Gentile or Muslim or Filipino or Canadian.

How can you meet the true Buddha sitting in the house?

FROM THE DIAMOND SUTRA:

"Thus I hear."

"All the Buddhas and the Buddhas' Dharma of the
Supreme Way arise from this sutra." What is this sutra?

"In this Dharma everything is equal;
There is neither high nor low."
Why is Mount Ro high and Mount An low?

"Dwelling nowhere, Mind comes forth."

"If you try to see me through colors
And to seek me through voices and sounds,
You are on a false path;
You will not be able to see the Tathagata."
How can you see the Tathagata?

Yuiho, *the dharma of phenomena.*
Muiho, *the dharma of emptiness.*

20

The full name of the discourse mentioned here is *The Diamond Sutra of the Perfection of Transcendental Wisdom*. The diamond cuts all other materials, but cannot itself be cut by any of them. When clean and polished, it shines resplendent in the tiniest light, even when immersed in water. Translating the title with this in mind, it could read, *The Discourse on the Penetration of the Impenetrable.*

The Diamond Sutra is part of the Prajna-Paramita Scriptures, the Wisdom Books, which came out of India, the "Guru of the World," as that country is often called. For the Northern Mahayana Buddhists, the Prajna-Paramita Scriptures are the most sacred and precious of all their canonical writing.

Prajna means the highest intuition, which views things in their aspect of *ku, shunyata,* emptiness. *Ku* is not nihilistic, but speaks of Ultimate Reality, which cannot be placed in any modern logical system. The Diamond Sutra sets forth the doctrine of *shunyata* (emptiness) and *prajna* (wisdom).

In this sutra the Buddha states that he does not have any fixed dharma to teach. His doctrine consists solely in wiping out all thoughts that stir the mind, so that the mind can be still. He says Wisdom, inherent in every person, can manifest itself and perceive the self-nature to come to Buddhahood.

In the introduction to the main body of the text we read:

> Now in the midst of the assembly was the Venerable Subhuti. [Subhuti was one of Shakyamuni's ten major disciples. He is depicted in the Hannya sutras as the foremost in understanding emptiness.] Forthwith Subhuti arose, uncovered his right shoulder, knelt upon his right knee, and respectfully raising his hands with palms joined, addressed Buddha thus: "World-Honored One, it is most precious how mindful the Tathagata is of all the bodhisattvas, protecting and instructing them so well! World-Honored One, if good men and good women seek the Consummation of Incomparable Enlightenment, by what criteria should they abide and how should they control their thought?"
>
> Buddha said, "Very good, Subhuti! Just as you say, the Tathagata is ever mindful of all the bodhisattvas, protecting and instructing them well. Now listen and take my words to heart: I will declare to you by what criteria good men and good women seeking the Consummation of Incomparable Enlightenment should abide, and how they should control their thoughts."

Subhuti said, "Pray, do, World-Honored One. With joyful anticipation we long to hear."

Now, presuming that you are all good men and women seeking the Consummation of Incomparable Enlightenment, we present the following excerpts from the Diamond Sutra to instruct you as to the criteria of how you should live and how you should control your thoughts.

"Thus I hear."
As background to this first phrase in the koan, I'd like to recall for you Shakyamuni's relative and constant companion during the last twenty years of his life, the man called Ananda, one of Buddha's ten great disciples.

Apparently, Shakyamuni's mother had died shortly after his birth, and her sister came to look after the infant. His father eventually married her, and Ananda is thought to be the child of that union.

It is recorded in the Buddhist books that Ananda was born during the very night Shakyamuni received his great enlightenment. Eventually he attached himself to the group of people who accompanied Shakyamuni on his mendicant preaching tours, and was a great favorite not only of the leader, but of the followers as well. He was a brilliant man with a most exceptional memory. He was called, "the best hearing and remembering monk." Whether because of his intellectual prowess or not, I cannot say, but the fact is that Ananda never had a satori experience during the lifetime of his famous relative. This must have bothered him, because we learn from Case 22 in the Mumonkan that he saw a non-Buddhist come to realization in dokusan with Shakyamuni, and he asked his cousin afterward, "What did that foreigner attain that made him praise you like that?"

Some years after Shakyamuni's death, a group of his enlightened disciples met for the purpose of compiling all their teacher's sermons. At this meeting, there was general consternation that Ananda could not be present, because he was as yet not enlightened. With his unusual memory, Ananda could quote from the sermons verbatim, and his presence was earnestly desired.

According to one story, Kashyapa, the leader of the group, put Ananda on a one-week's sesshin, and then examined him. Ananda was able to come to realization, and therefore qualified to participate in the gathering. He recited from memory all of the sermons, starting each with the phrase, "Thus have I heard." And that is why many of the sutras begin with these words: Thus have I heard.

Now show me! How do you hear?

"All the Buddhas and the Buddhas' Dharma of the Supreme Way arise from this sutra." What is this sutra?
All through the sutra, there is an insistence on the teaching, "All those who seek the Consummation of the Incomparable Enlightenment should discipline their thoughts." Also, "no bodhisattva who is a real bodhisattva cherishes the idea of an ego-entity, a personality, a being, or a separated individuality."

When we think "ego," we solidify it as against its opposite, "non-ego." In the same way, "being" poses "non-being"; the use of "I" separates into "I" and "all else." This is the way our bifurcating intellect works. Only in the transcendent state, beyond opposites, is the Infinite realized. So what is this sutra? It can't be the opposite to "that" sutra. How do you transcend *this* sutra and *that* sutra? There is another section of the sutra not quoted in this koan that says the Infinite is undeclarable! If that is so, then how are you going to transcend the opposite to declare the Infinite, which is undeclarable?

Remember Moses contemplating the burning bush that would not be consumed, and the emanating voice that told him what to do. "Who are you, anyway?" Moses demanded. He wanted a name to set this Infinite apart from all others—and the answer he got was "I am who am," which in Hebrew turned out to be Yahweh, a verb: *am*. How sad that we often replace God's own revelation of himself as *dynamic* with our own static images—we have stripped God of vitality and given him a long white beard, sitting on a throne in heaven! Where is heaven?

But most particularly—what is this sutra?

"In this Dharma everything is equal; there is neither high nor low." Why is Mount Ro high and Mount An low?
The English word *equal* tends to be bifurcating—one thing has the same measure, quantity, amount, or number as another; another case of this and that, you and I, etc. But *equal* also means regarding or affecting all objects in the same way, which concur in the Dharma. By its very nature, the Dharma sees all as equal. Why then is one mountain high and one low?

I trust there is no serious Zen student who would present this koan in dokusan as a study in comparative topography! Nor do we sit on a celestial throne and proclaim all mountains are the same. (Sometimes Yamada Roshi would draw a circle of the earth with the two mountains visible, one higher than the other. Since both mountains *are* the universe, whether you start with Mount An or Mount Ro, it doesn't make any difference—the total circumference is the same. In other words, totally they are the same height.) In the Diamond Sutra, Buddha tells us that a bodhisattva does not discover through an intellectual process. Why? Because, he says, "If men allow their minds to grasp and hold on to anything, they would be cherishing the idea of an ego-entity, a personality, a being, or a separated individuality. Likewise, if they grasped and held on to the notion of things as devoid of intrinsic qualities, they would still be cherishing the idea of an ego-entity, a personality, a being, or a separated individuality. So you should not be attached to things as being possessed of, or devoid of, intrinsic qualities."

It is at this point in his teaching that the Buddha refers to his teaching about a raft. A question is asked, "Does a man who has safely crossed a flood upon a raft continue his journey carrying that raft upon his head?" So long as the mind is attached even to Buddha's teaching, as a basis, it will cherish the idea of *I* and *other.*

After the Buddha stated that we should not be attached to things as being possessed of or devoid of intrinsic qualities, he said, "This is the reason why the Tathagata always teaches this saying, 'My teaching of the Good Law is to be likened unto a raft. The Buddha-teaching must be relinquished—thrown away! How much more mis-teaching!'"

Now let us return to our two mountains. Please sidestep all mis-teaching, and show me why Mount Ro is high, and Mount An is low.

"Dwelling nowhere, Mind comes forth."

The Diamond Sutra says Subhuti abides nowhere. In another place in the discourse, the Buddha says, "If the mind depends upon anything, it has no sure haven." But before I discuss the sutra text, I'd like to give a parallel text in the New Testament: "Foxes have holes, and birds have nests, but the Son of Man has no place to lie down and rest." (Luke 5:58) This is usually cited to underline Jesus' poor and simple life. It seems to me Jesus is exhorting us to real detachment as well—to be free from all attachments.

"Subhuti dwells nowhere; therefore he is cited, 'Subhuti, Joyful-Abider-in-Peace, Dweller-in-Seclusion-in-the-forest.'" Dweller in seclusion in the forest has a double meaning. It can mean an ascetic hermitage, and dwelling aloof and immune from distraction and temptation in the dark forest tangle of human perplexities and desires.* (So Buddha says, "Cut down the whole forest, not just a single tree…Cut down the great trees and clear away the undergrowth; then monks, will you be free from the forest."

Dwelling nowhere, your mind must come forth. Our mind is our consciousness. Can we tell where it is? (Some people point to their head, but that is the brain they're referring to!) In reality, we can't locate it! And yet we can see it function. And as Yamada Roshi used to say, "It is the entrance to the essence of the vast, limitless universe." Because his teaching is excellent on this point, let me continue:

We cannot locate our essential nature, because it is zero, yet it has infinite capabilities. It can see with eyes, walk with legs, think with a brain, and digest food with a stomach. It weeps when it is sad, and laughs when it is happy. Though it is zero, no one can deny its existence. It is one with phenomena. The essential nature and phenomena are one from the very beginning. That is why the *Hannya Shingyo* [or the Heart Sutra] can say, "Form is nothing but emptiness, emptiness is nothing but form."**

If your mind must come forth, show it to me! Right here! Right now! Let me see! Well, well, well!

"If you try to see me through colors, and to seek me through voices and sounds, you are on a false path; you will not be able to see the Tathagata." How can you see the Tathagata?
In the Diamond Sutra, the Buddha asks, "What do you think? Is the Tathagata to be recognized by some material characteristics? Wherefore? Because the Tathagata has said that material characteristics are not, in fact, material characteristics." He continued, "Wheresoever are material characteristics, there is delusion; but whosoever perceives that all characteristics are in fact no-characteristics, perceives the Tathagata."

One translation of the sutra puts it this way: "That is to say, he should practice compassion without regard to appearances; without regard to sound, odor, touch, flavor, or any quality." And later, Buddha says,

* Cf. *The Dhammapada* 20–283.
** Koun Yamada, *The Gateless Gate*, (Boston: Wisdom Publications, 2004), 28–29

"Therefore, all bodhisattvas, lesser and great, should develop a pure lucid mind, not depending upon sound, flavor, touch, odor, or any quality. A bodhisattva should develop a mind which alights upon no-thing whatsoever; and so should he establish it." Perhaps this is mindfulness.

And how like John of the Cross he sounds in the final utterance of section 26 of the sutra:

> *Who seeks Me by form,*
> *Who seeks Me in sound,*
> *Perverted are his footsteps upon the Way;*
> *For he cannot perceive the Tathagata!*

Or as C.S. Lewis says in his book, *Letters to Malcolm:* "Every idea of Him we form, He must in mercy shatter."

Following that in the text, there is the departure of the disciple Subhuti, and there are comments on the reason. Did the Venerable Subhuti leave? Why? Or is it a faulty text? For me there is no wonder: what would you do if your teacher said: "Who seeks Me by form / Who seeks Me in sound / Perverted are his footsteps upon the Way; / For he cannot perceive the Tathagata"?

I suspect Subhuti just put on his seven paneled robes and left! I'm glad, though, that none of you have followed in his footsteps, because I want to ask you. How do you meet the Tathagata?

Yuiho, the dharma of phenomena.

Yuiho points to the dharma of form and shape. We are taught in the sutra that all phenomenal things are under the law of change. They are like a dream, a phantom, a bubble, a shadow. They are like dew, or a flash of lightning. You should see things like this.

> *Thus shall ye think of all this fleeting world:*
> *A star at dawn, a bubble in a stream,*
> *A flash of lightning in a summer cloud,*
> *A flickering lamp, a phantom and a dream.*

Muiho, the dharma of emptiness.

Muiho, the dharma of emptiness, with no beginning or no end. The word *muiho* implies effortlessness, all things are freely subject to emptiness.

The first mentioned is the Diamond Prajna-Paramita, which is in the genre of Wisdom literature, and conveys the message of the dharma.

The muiho dharma? Self-nature, self-realization, Essential Nature, satori, enlightenment, Buddha Nature, Heaven, Lotus Land, Nirvana, etc. They have no shape or form, even though they are in our phenomenal world.

In daily life, we are always meeting and seeing Tathagata. Every moment, every task we do, life itself, is replete with fullness and emptiness. We live each second as a minute, each minute as hour, each hour as a day, each day as a week, and each month as a year. Each moment is a lifetime. Let us live each moment replete with fullness and emptiness. The following story seems to illustrate the process in the midst of completion.

> Once upon a time there was a Chinese carpenter whose work was so extraordinary that the Prince of Lu called him in and said to him, "These things you make are so perfect that it does not seem possible that any human being could make them. Is it true or is it not true that in your work you have superhuman assistance?" And Ching, the carpenter, who was a very humble man, answered the Prince of Lu something like this: "First of all, when I am to make some cabinet or box of great quality, I separate myself from the world for two days. At the end of that time, I am no longer aware of title, dignity, or estate, so that no matter for whom I am making this box, I am just making it for a person. There is no longer any glamor, no longer any sense that I must make a better box because a great nobleman has ordered it. Then for two days more, I relax and meditate, and I come to the conclusion that it is of no consequence whether the box is good or bad. I no longer fear that my work will not be sufficient; I no longer hope that it will be outstanding. I have lost all interest in whether I am praised or blamed for the thing I have produced. Then, in two days more, I am no longer aware of myself. I no longer care whether I exist or not. Gradually, that part of my mind that is naturally and usually devoted to personal concerns is relaxed away from these, so that I no longer know that I have a body or that I have hands or feet. Everything becomes very quiet. All this time I have been visualizing what I am going to build,

until finally there is nothing but visualization and the object. Having attained this degree of internal rapport with value, I then go out into the forest, or wherever the materials for the object are to be found, and I wander about until I find my piece of work—my box or cabinet or screen—somewhere within the body of something that already exists. I look at a tree and I say, 'There is my box.' I look at bamboo and say, 'There is my screen.' And I am aware that I am going to move the box that is already in the tree out of the tree where it can be seen. Then I sit down quietly with all my materials, and I allow Heaven to put the box together. When Heaven puts the box together, the seams are perfect. When men put a box together, the seams are not perfect because a man will say, 'This seam is better than that seam,' or, 'I must make a good seam,' or, 'Will the purchaser be pleased with the box?' Thus all things come to nothing. But I am concerned only with the fact that Heaven makes a box, and the box that Heaven makes will please Heaven, and if I am fortunate in all these matters, the box I have made will cause the Prince of Lu to say to me, 'Did you receive superhuman help?'"

In our daily lives, we work with objects, boundaries, and other elements seen as contradictions to Tathagata. But discipline and practice bring all things to me.

The way of the Buddha is intrinsically accomplished and perfect.

The principle of Buddhism is complete freedom.

If there is only a bit of difference,
it is the distance between heaven and earth.

Attainment of the Way, realization of mind;
Just putting your head through the gate.

Non-thinking.

You may practice Zen and get enlightenment
But IT, by its nature, is never tainted by such matters.
When you practice Zen upward (step by step), every step is
equal in substance.

21

Dogen Zenji was the man Thomas Merton called his kindred spirit. He was the founder of the Soto lineage in Japan, of which stream we in the Sanbo Kyodan are a part, and he is especially revered by teachers in all branches of Zen now, although he was unappreciated for many years because his teachings were (and still are) often misunderstood.

Dogen was born in Kyoto, January 2, 1200, within the court circle of the day. His father, a descendant of the Emperor Murakami, died when Dogen was only two years old. Dogen was raised in a culturally over-refined atmosphere, systematically educated in the Japanese and Chinese classics, and trained in literary skills and techniques. He said, "In my childhood, I studied history and literature enthusiastically." He was always very sensitive to language, and wrote an instruction *"Ago"*— "Living Speech."

Dogen's mother was Motofusa, the daughter of the dominating Fuji- wara family. She died when he was seven years old. At her death, she left him an earnest request to seek the truth by becoming a monk, in which life he could help relieve the tragic sufferings of humanity. Her death was a serious blow to his fragile and sensitive mind. We are told that in the midst of profound grief, Dogen experienced the imperma- nence of all things, as he watched the ascending incense at his mother's funeral service.

When he was twelve, he opted to become a monk. He was ordained at Enryakuji on Mount Hiei, in 1213. He did a systematic study of the sutras. No more favorable educational environment could be found in his day than on Mount Hiei. Dogen devoured these studies with his gifted mind. On February 22, 1223, he set out for China.

Dogen found the teaching in the various Zen temples there very uneven. For some time, he lived on board the vessel in which he had sailed, and visited many of the teachers. Strangely enough, he was most impressed by a Zen monk who came to the ship to buy Japanese mush- rooms. He was the *tenzo* (head cook) of his monastery, and Dogen found the answers to his questions very satisfying. One day, he tried to get the cook engaged in long conversation, but the cook was in a hurry to return. Dogen chided him that anyone could cook, and it would be better for him to stay on the ship for a while longer. The monk replied that cook- ing was his practice and no one could do his practice for him. Dogen learned much from this tenzo, and was later ashamed of himself for what he had said. So he decided to go to the monk's temple to meet his teacher.

It was May 1, 1225, that Dogen met Ju-ching, who was a warm and loving father to him. He made himself available to the young Japanese monk, and this availability rekindled the young inquiring mind with a burning desire for truth. He was later to say, "If you don't meet the right master, it is better not to study Zen at all." And he thereafter held the belief that it is absolutely necessary to have personal encounter with a teacher in Zen practice.

During *Ango* (an intensive training period) in 1225, he heard what was said to some sleepy monks, "In zazen, it is imperative to cast off body and mind. How could you indulge in sleeping?" This shook Dogen to the core. He broke out into a sweat, and rushed to the master's room, lit a stick of incense, and prostrated himself. When asked to speak, he could only reply, "Body and mind fallen away." It is recorded that the master demanded of him, "Show me the fallen away body and mind." Dogen's presentation was accepted. In 1228 he returned to Kyoto and wrote the *Fukan Zazengi*.

Dogen Zenji lived in the early half of the Kamakura era (1192–1333), a time when radical societal changes were underway. Japan, burdened with imitating the political and social pattern of the T'ang Dynasty in China, began shaking itself free from the troublesome formalism of its aristocratic government, and moving toward a military one.

Traditional Buddhism, a religion for nobles, had degenerated into a kind of esoteric practice or collection of magical rites. In contrast to this, the Buddhism of this new age celebrated a return to its fundamentals, directing itself toward becoming easily attainable and simply understood. Zen was one of the three main sects central to this new Buddhism.

Dogen's Soto sect accentuated zazen more than anything else. In particular, he advocated *shikantaza*, "just sitting": a single-minded sitting in zazen. Among the plethora of teachings, it may be argued that Dogen's shows the strongest tendency to return to the true, original spirit of Buddha, where an appeal is made to fluid and direct intuition, rather than static and rigid logic. A person arrives at the wisdom of Buddhism not as a result of logical reasoning but through enlightenment experiences, which, however, do not negate the intellect. Dogen does not ignore the need for the mind to be continually refined through sitting; and he says that when, through refining, the mind returns to its pure, original spontaneity, it will always be able to exercise this wisdom appropriately. He writes in *Fukan Zazengi*: "Assisting the mind to return to its original state is of the essence of zazen."

Dogen's *Fukan Zazengi* is his manifesto of Soto Zen for Japan, in which he explains shikantaza as a practice of sitting, by which the mind is set free and returned to the state of its activity as a pure "liberated" spirit. If the student wants this inner spirit always to be acting appropriately, the practice of zazen must be continued without interruption. He taught that enlightenment is always concerned with practice—that shikantaza is zazen for zazen's sake—just sit in zazen. As you can imagine, such simplicity can be easily misconstrued. Over the centuries, his great erudition, his concern for people and society, and his religious stature were reduced to quips; and in contemporary Japan, Soto monks preach that Dogen had no use for satori, that dokusan and teisho are also useless, and it suffices only to sit. Without going into detail, let me say that in the last century, Dogen's true teaching has reappeared and his difficult works are slowly being understood more deeply.

The koans we deal with here are some excerpts from the *Fukan Zazengi,* which he wrote immediately after his return from China.

The way of the Buddha is intrinsically accomplished and perfect.

It is characteristic of Dogen's writing style to say the most important things first. The whole *Fukan Zazengi* starts with three Japanese words, *Tazunuru ni sore,* which can be approximately translated as, "After earnestly searching..." Yasutani Roshi said that his teacher, Harada Roshi, used to stress the significance of the opening words. They are reminiscent of Eka's search in his encounter with Bodhidharma, "I have searched for it, and *finally* I cannot find it." In varying degrees, this is true for us all.

The sense of the opening passage is something like, "After searching exhaustingly for the truth, he came to the realization that the very essence of the Way is originally perfect and all-pervading." The word translated as *originally* is not only an adverb; but the same character could also be translated as a noun; the "origin of the Way" or "the fundamental Way." And why is it said to be the fundamental Way? It is because it is universal, it is all-pervading, it is complete. So I ask you: what is it?

All of us are here to find our True Self or the real implication of life and death. But here it says, "After searching exhaustingly, the very essence or origin of the Way is perfect and all-pervading." What is the Way? *Supreme enlightenment.* In Chinese, it's translated as the Supreme Way, the very best Way, the Unsurpassable Way, or as perfect Wisdom— which is what enlightenment actually is. Thus enlightenment is synonymous with the Way.

Again we may ask, "What is wisdom?" It is our life itself.

We not only have that wisdom, we are constantly using it. When it's cold, we put on more clothing. When it's hot, we take layers off. When hungry, we eat. When sad, we cry. Being happy, we laugh. That's wisdom. And it doesn't only pertain to humans either, but to anything and everything. Birds chirp, dogs run, mountains are high, valleys are low. It's all wisdom! The seasons change, the stars shine in the heavens—

wisdom! Regardless of whether we realize it or not, we are always in the midst of the Way. Or more strictly speaking we are nothing but the Way itself.

Of course there are always reasons and causes for our being the way we are. So the key is how clearly we realize the Way, which is, after all, nothing but ourselves. And realizing the Way is all-pervading, perfect, and complete. What do we have to worry about? In the Soto School, our emphasis is more on this original realization or fundamental enlightenment, *which is nothing but our life itself.* Then what we should do is take care of it and not stain or defile it. Whatever we do then becomes the act of the Buddha. (A friend, Father Yves Raguin, S.J., says, "Whatever we do is an act of God.")

That's what the first line refers to when it says, "The Way is complete and all-pervading." How could it be contingent on practice and realization?

The principle of Buddhism is complete freedom.
Norman Waddell and Masao Abe's translation of this line says, "The Dharma-Vehicle is free and untrammeled." Actually here Dogen is saying the same thing again. The vehicle, this very essence of life, is totally free, without bondage or restriction, and this vehicle is nothing but our life. It is originally free, unrestricted. Of course, as long as we are alive, we live under certain conditions, which, in a sense, is a limitation. But within limitation, there is always freedom.

As we say about Manjusri who, in Case 42 of the Mumonkan, cannot awaken the woman in samadhi by snapping his fingers, "I'm not free to be a man, but I'm not unfree in my own state." If you concentrate on your nonfreedom, on your restriction, you'll be miserable! Regardless of where you go or what you do, in one way or another your life is restricted. Looking to circumstances or the environment for your freedom is the wrong attitude. You always find freedom *within* limitation.

Our original self, our essential nature, or whatever else we call it—that is the Way, and it's free and all-pervading. The *Fukan Zazengi* (in a part not quoted in this koan) goes on to say that "it is never apart from one, right where one is. What is the use of going off here and there to practice?" IT is very important. IT is always here. IT is always right now. And IT is the same for all. Always, wherever you go, where you are, IT is right here, right now, complete, free, all-pervading. Isn't it wonderful? This is our life. So just be so; be so. Don't defile it or stain it.

If there is only a bit of difference, it is the distance between heaven and earth.

And I'd like to add the next sentence, which, although it does not appear in this koan, is another way of saying the same thing: "*If the least like or dislike arises, the mind is lost in confusion.*"

If there is even the least shadow of concept, it is miles and miles away from Mu. So eliminate or set aside those ideas and preconceived notions. Just stop that entire process of analyzing an idea formation.

When you have ideas of liking or disliking, right or wrong, good or bad, enlightened or deluded, then you lose the mind. In dichotomy, you become apart from the Way.

Attainment of the Way, realization of mind; Just putting your head through the gate.

In our orientation talks, we describe satori as a treasure contained in a palace surrounded by a walled fortress. Until we have kensho, we are just walking around the outside of the walls. With kensho, we make a wee break in the wall, usually just enough to get our head through. After that, we have to get the whole body through, and then proceed through the grounds to the house, and then to the innermost room, where the treasure is kept. We say, "the head is through, but the body is still sticking out." In other words it is still a very immature and early stage. Attaining enlightenment, clear vision, wisdom, seeing that the whole world is nothing but myself—such understanding is nothing but the beginning. Don't get stuck there or you'll never liberate yourself. Dogen Zenji says that even having had clear glimpse of enlightenment and feeling elated, it can become a pleasant memory only. The Zen process is a lifetime work. We are never entirely free. He is telling us that we must be careful about how we proceed in our practice. He warns us against attaining a little bit of realization and getting prematurely satisfied and conceited. To the extent that we do so, we tie ourselves up and become unfree.

Non-thinking.

From the *Fukan Zazengi*, the longer statement is: "*Do not think good or bad. Do not administer pros and cons. Cease all the movements of the conscious mind, the gauging of all thoughts and views.*"

At least when we sit we should put thoughts aside. That's what it means. But this doesn't imply that Dogen denies the value of consciousness. He isn't urging us merely to become like logs or stones. Without any thoughts or views, our consciousness can still clearly function. That's why the surface of the mind is compared to that of a very clear, bright mirror. We cannot say that if there is no reflection, there is no mirror. The mirror is there, and simply reflects whatever is before it. Whatever comes up is clearly shown, and when the object vanishes, so does the reflection. Not a trace remains behind. Nothing sticking to it. That's the state of mind we're supposed to maintain during the practice of zazen. But it's hard. It is not easy.

Harada Roshi used to say that shikantaza is putting yourself into a state of non-thinking and sitting strong.

You may practice Zen and get enlightenment but *IT*, by its nature, is never tainted by such matters.
Self-centered, ego-centered ideas are what create defilement. All of us are using wisdom constantly. When the time comes to get up, we get up; when the time comes, we eat. Everything goes smoothly. It's wisdom, not only for the human, but for everything else. But somehow or other, we mix it all up, and don't do what needs doing. Ideally, whatever comes along, day after day, we just put ourselves into it.

Then, "practice-realization" is naturally undefiled. "Going forward in practice is a matter of everydayness"—this is one of the most important statements in the *Fukan Zazengi*. Going forward, regardless of how far we achieve or we accomplish, still it's ordinary. Regardless of how far we go, still it's everyday. "Everyday" sounds a little awkward. I prefer the word *ordinary*—which is etymologically derived from the Latin word meaning "order." Orderliness is extremely important. Orderliness of mind, orderliness of body, orderliness of daily life, orderliness of even our room, surroundings, orderliness of groups, orderliness of society, country, everything. That's supposed to be ordinary. Then there's no problem no matter how far we go, we are just whatever we are. So we don't need to lose our heads, or acquire an extra one. Ordinary. We can live our life like that, and there will be no problems. Then practice-realization is naturally undefiled. This is one of the instances where Dogen Zenji is misunderstood when he said the *IT*, the Essential Nature, is always the same, whether before enlightenment or afterward. Substantially there is no change. Whether you get enlightenment or not, your Essential Nature is the same.

When you practice Zen upward (step by step), every step is equal in substance.

The notes on the section above said there are no steps in Zen, but here we say there are. "There are stages, there are no stages" is an old Zen saying. When you practice Zen, for instance koan study, one step by one step, you are advancing, so there are steps; but then from the Essential point of view, before kensho, after kensho, before *daigotetei* (a very deep kensho experience), and after, it's all the same—so there are no steps.

Although not part of our koan, Dogen Zenji finishes his *Fukan Zazengi:* "Devote your energies to a Way that directly indicates the absolute...your treasure-store will open of itself, and you will use it at will."

That's the conclusion of the *Fukan Zazengi:* "Your treasure house will open of itself, and you will use it at will." Again it goes back to the very beginning, "The Way is perfect and all-pervading." That Way is the treasure house. And the Dharma-vehicle is free and untrammeled. It's nothing but ourselves."

Appreciate yourself!! And don't let your treasure house be filled by fighting spirits and warring factions, but shared with Buddhas and Bodhisattvas and Patriarchs of today and the past and the future.

HARYO'S THREE TURNING WORDS

What is the Deva Sect?
"Piling up snow in a silver bowl."

What is the Way?
"The clearly enlightened monk falls into a well."

What is the sharpest sword?
"The dew on the top of each branch of coral reflects the light
of the moon."

22

Here we have another set of turning words. Haryo was a disciple of the famous teacher, Unmon. At the time of transmission, Unmon was supposed to present a certificate to Haryo, but instead, Haryo presented his teacher with these three turning words. Unmon was so delighted, he said, "When I die, I do not want a funeral service. Instead, dedicate a teisho to me on these three turning words!"

What is the Deva Sect? "Piling up snow in a silver bowl."
The Deva in this koan is the fifteenth ancestor after Shakyamuni, whom we find in the Master Keizan's Denkoroku, *The Record of Transmitting the Light.* His full name is Kanadeva, and he came from a very rich family. He worked in the family banking business, and he was famous not for wealth but for debate. The *Gomyo,* the five branches of learning in ancient India, made a philosopher out of everyone, and Kanadeva, an exceptionally bright and intelligent man,

was outstanding. He challenged everyone to debate, and always suc-
ceeded in vanquishing them. He seemed unbeatable in disputation.

And then one day, he met the Venerable Nagarjuna and the story
changed. Challenged to debate by this eminent Buddhist, Deva did the
best he could, but it wasn't good enough. For the first time in his life he
was completely defeated, and begged to become a disciple of his opponent. In due time, he entered the Buddhist priesthood.

And then he started philosophical debating as a Buddhist priest. Some
scholars say there were at least ninety-six different schools of philosophy
in India at that time. So Deva must have been busy, and, it is said, as a
Buddhist priest he defeated all the philosophers who debated with him.

In those days, the winner of a debate would announce victory by
raising a red flag, and the loser would have to sit under the flag. In
extreme cases, the loser would cut off his arm or even his own head in
shame. Once when Deva defeated an opponent in an argument, the
latter in shame was going to cut off his own head (don't ask me how!)
when Deva stopped him. In gratitude the man become his disciple and
shaved his head to become a priest. And this was the beginning of the
Deva Sect.

According to some scholars, the Zen Sect is in the line of the Deva
Sect. The word *zen* does not appear in Buddhism until after Bodhidharma went to China. According to Yamada Roshi, what is now called
the Zen Sect was first called the Shobogenzo Sect—The Right Dharma-
Eye Treasury, which Shakyamuni is supposed to have used when he
transmitted the Dharma to Mahakasyapa. Then the sect was called the
Deva Sect. Later, when Bodhidharma went to China, it was called the
Bodhidharma Sect. The fourth identifying name was the Sokei Sect,
named after the mountain where Master Eno stayed. And the fifth name
was Rinzai Sect (and probably its twin, Soto Sect).

Anyway, when we ask, "What is the Deva Sect?" we are asking "What
is Zen?" or "What is the primal face?" or "Why did the Patriarch come
from the West?" In other words, we are asking the eternal question.

In this koan, we have a monk asking Haryo, "What is the Deva
Sect?" And Haryo answering, "Heaping up snow in a silver bowl."
What a beautiful concise reply! Ordinarily a Zen person doesn't have
a lot to say about the essence of Zen. As Bodhidharma said, "It is not
connected with words and letters, being a special transmission outside
of teaching." Dogen Zenji has said, "Having no connection with words
and letters, what can be said about all words and letters?"

In the Hekiganroku, the second sentence of the Instruction says, "Snow covers the reed blossoms, and it is hard to distinguish the slightest trace of them." The blossoms of reed are white. White snow has fallen on the white blossoms—they are the same color. Looking carefully, though, we see that snow is snow and blossoms are blossoms. The difference is there, but since both are white, it is difficult to distinguish. Snow is white, and the silver bowl becomes white. These are the same in their whiteness. But snow is not silver, silver is not snow. The same but different. Different but the same.

And we have the talented philosopher Deva, debating successfully; and the converted Buddhist priest, still a talented philosopher, also debating successfully. Like the snow and the reed blossoms, and like the snow reflected on the sides of a silver bowl, Deva was the same but different, different but the same. You must therefore give a presentation in dokusan of two things that are similar but different from each other, different from each other but the same.

What is the Way? "The clearly enlightened monk falls into a well."
What is the Way? The ordinary mind is the way. No mind is the way. "If your bowls are dirty, wash them" is the Way. Tokusan carries his bowls is the Way. Clattering your bowls at mealtime is the Way. "Please don't"—is the Way. Nanzen killing a cat and Tozan's sixty blows is the Way. The *kaimeito* tree in the front garden—is the Way.

But, you may perhaps say, this part of the teisho is starting to sound like the table of contents of the Mumonkan. Precisely! And I think of the remarks an American disciple made to Yamada Roshi as she was doing the Miscellaneous Koans after kensho—"They are all the same question!" she laughingly remarked.

"What is the Way?" "What is Zen?" "What is Reality?" "What is the True Self?" "What is the Essential Nature?"

Right now! Right here! The fact!

What is the Way when the clearly enlightened monk falls into a well? What is the True Self when the clearly enlightened monk falls into a well? What is the Essential Nature when the clearly enlightened monk falls into a well? The fact is a million miles away from the concept. There are some who think the fact can be contained in the concept. That's how erroneous "thinking" can be, in Zen. Haryo has a little hook...the koan means "This is the Way the clearly enlightened monk falls into a well." What is that "Way?"

What is the sharpest sword? "The dew on the top of each branch of coral reflects the light of the moon."

Down in Leyte, in the Philippines, there is a lot of coral. As Haryo says, sometimes the coral has many branches, sometimes the shape of a large mushroom or a spray of fern—a great cluster of tiny branches, delicately intertwined like a piece of intricate lace! Then, when the moonlight (which is of course the Essential Nature) shines on the drop of dew on the tip of each branch—it's just like...*Katsu!*

The branches are the many aspects of the world we see—the body, the mountain, grass, walls, floor, etc. The branches are also the many aspects of the world we cannot see—sweet, sour, beautiful, dirty, happy, sad. They are also aspects of the world of concepts, the everyday world, (dark and light, right and wrong); the world of relationships (boss and employee, husband and wife, roshi and me); the world of delusion (in Buddhism there are six), etc. And through all these, the light of the moon, the light of the Essential Nature, which is the trunk, shines!

And I cannot help presenting a very comforting and beautiful Christian parallel. "I am the vine, you are the branches. Whoever remains in me, and I in him, will bear much fruit; for you can do nothing without me. I love you, just as the Father loves me: remain in my love...I have told you this, so that my joy may be in you, and that your joy may be complete." (John 15:5–11)

"The dew on the top of each branch of coral reflects the light of the moon."

What do you suppose this has to do with the sharpest sword?

Glossary of Japanese Words

ango intensive training period

bodhisattva a person who seeks enlightenment but delays full enlightenment until all beings are saved; a saint

Buppo Buddha-dharma; the teaching of Shakyamuni

daigotetei a very deep kensho experience

dhyana the Sanskrit word for meditation, which comes to us as *zen*

dojo the place of practice

dokusan the private interview between the student and the teacher

Hekiganroku "The Blue Cliff Record"; a collection of one hundred koans

joriki the power of the concentrated mind

kanji Japanese ideograms

Katsu! a shout that is meant to help the student achieve a breakthrough

kensho "seeing one's true nature"; an enlightenment experience

kensho-ki a kensho diary; a written account of one's kensho experience

kinhin walking meditation

kokoro our most intimate inner place

kotsu a teacher's stick that is a sign of confirmation of transmission

mondo questions and answers; Zen repartee

Muji the koan Mu

mudra hand position

Mumonkan "The Gateless Gate"; perhaps the most famous collection of koans

roshi teacher

sangha community of disciples

satori enlightenment

sesshin a meditation retreat that lasts for several days, usually seven or ten

shitsunai shirabe program of koan study with a Zen master (literally, "in-the-room investigation")

shoken a student's first interview with the teacher

teisho a Zen talk

zazen sitting meditation

zazenkai a day-long meditation retreat

About Wisdom Publications

Wisdom Publications, a nonprofit publisher, is dedicated to making available authentic works relating to Buddhism for the benefit of all. We publish books by ancient and modern masters in all traditions of Buddhism, translations of important texts, and original scholarship. Additionally, we offer books that explore East-West themes unfolding as traditional Buddhism encounters our modern culture in all its aspects. Our titles are published with the appreciation of Buddhism as a living philosophy, and with the special commitment to preserve and transmit important works from Buddhism's many traditions.

To learn more about Wisdom, or to browse books online, visit our website at www.wisdompubs.org.

You may request a copy of our catalog online or by writing to this address:

Wisdom Publications
199 Elm Street
Somerville, Massachusetts 02144 USA
Telephone: 617-776-7416
Fax: 617-776-7841
Email: info@wisdompubs.org
www.wisdompubs.org

THE WISDOM TRUST

As a nonprofit publisher, Wisdom is dedicated to the publication of Dharma books for the benefit of all sentient beings and dependent upon the kindness and generosity of sponsors in order to do so. If you would like to make a donation to Wisdom, you may do so through our website or our Somerville office. If you would like to help sponsor the publication of a book, please write or email us at the address above. Thank you.

Wisdom is a nonprofit, charitable 501(c)(3) organization affiliated with the Foundation for the Preservation of the Mahayana Tradition (FPMT).

Other books of interest by Wisdom Publications

Sitting With Koans
Essential Writings on the Practice of Zen Koan Introspection
Edited by John Daido Loori
Introduction by Thomas Yuho Kirchner
352 pp, ISBN 0-86171-296-X, $16.95

"This collection of classic writings on koans will get you started and open up the treasure in your own heart."—John Tarrant, author of *Bring Me the Rhinoceros (And Other Zen Koans to Bring You Joy)*

"A remarkable collection brilliantly put together by a premier modern interpreter of koans."—Steven Heine, author of *The Zen Canon: Understanding Classic Texts*

The Gateless Gate
The Classic Book of Zen Koans
Koun Yamada
Foreword by Ruben L.F. Habito
288 pages, ISBN 0-86171-382-6, $16.95

"The penetrating voice of a unique lay Zen master! The depth of Yamada Koun Roshi's insight doesn't allow him to keep any religious, cultural or racial border in his heart. Consequently many Westerners as well as Catholics have joined his sangha. Reading his words, we realize that the Dharma has nothing to do with east or west, Buddhism or Christianity. Buddha nature is universal."—Eido Shimano Roshi, Abbot of Dai Bosatsu Zendo, Kongo-Ji